ROBOTIC PROCESS AUTOMATION
AND ITS APPLICATIONS

Matthew N. O. Sadiku, Ph.D., P.E.

Regents Professor Emeritus and IEEE Life Fellow

Prairie View A&M University

Prairie View, TX 77446

Email: sadiku@ieee.org

Web: www.matthew-sadiku.com

Robotic Process Automation

ISBN: 979-8-2560-0966-3

Edition: Hardcover

Copyright: 1-15160909851

Library of Congress Control Number: 2026912778

Permissions Notice: write to the author at: sadiku@ieee.org

Printed and published in the USA

Author's Website: https://matthew-sadiku.com/

Publisher Information:

SELFPUBLISHINGLLC

Published by Self-Publishing LLC | SelfPublishingLLC.com

Credits

Publisher: Steve Martin

DEDICATED TO MY WIFE:
JANET O. SADIKU

ABOUT THE AUTHOR

Matthew N. O. Sadiku received his B. Sc. degree in 1978 from Ahmadu Bello University, Zaria, Nigeria and his M.Sc. and Ph.D. degrees from Tennessee Technological University, Cookeville, TN in 1982 and 1984 respectively. From 1984 to 1988, he was an assistant professor at Florida Atlantic University, Boca Raton, FL, where he did graduate work in computer science. In total, he received seven college degrees. From 1988 to 2000, he was at Temple University, Philadelphia, PA, where he became a full professor. From 2000 to 2002, he was with Lucent/Avaya, Holmdel, NJ as a system engineer and with Boeing Satellite Systems, Los Angeles, CA as a senior scientist. He is presently a Regents professor emeritus of electrical and computer engineering at Prairie View A&M University, Prairie View, TX.

He is the author of over 1,600 professional papers and over 170 books including "Elements of Electromagnetics" (Oxford University Press, 7th ed., 2018), "Fundamentals of Electric Circuits" (McGraw-Hill, 7th ed., 2020, with C. Alexander), "Computational Electromagnetics with MATLAB" (CRC Press, 4th ed., 2019), "Principles of Modern Communication Systems" (Cambridge University Press, 2017, with S. O. Agbo), and "Emerging Internet-based Technologies" (CRC Press, 2019). In addition to the engineering books, he has written Christian books including "Secrets of Successful

Marriages" (with J. O. Sadiku), "How to Discover God's Will for Your Life," and commentaries on all the books of the New Testament Bible. Some of his books have been translated into ten languages: French, Korean, Chinese (and Chinese Long Form in Taiwan), Italian, Portuguese, Spanish, German, Dutch, Polish, and Russian.

He was the recipient of the 2000 McGraw-Hill/Jacob Millman Award for outstanding contributions in the field of electrical engineering. He was also the recipient of Regents Professor award for 2012-2013 by the Texas A&M University System. He is a registered professional engineer and a life fellow of the Institute of Electrical and Electronics Engineers (IEEE) "for contributions to computational electromagnetics and engineering education." He is also a Fellow of the Nigerian Academy of Engineering (NAE). He was the IEEE Region 2 Student Activities Committee Chairman. He was an associate editor for IEEE Transactions on Education. He is also a member of Association for Computing Machinery (ACM). His current research interests are in the areas of computational electromagnetic, computer science/networks, engineering education, and marriage counseling. His works can be found in his autobiography, "My Life and Work" (Trafford Publishing, 2024) or his website: www.matthew-sadiku.com. He can be reached via email at sadiku@ieee.org

PREFACE

Robotic process automation (RPA) is a software technology that facilitates the development and management of software that simulates human actions while interfacing with digitized systems. It is a part of digital transformation since it enables businesses to automate procedures, increase accuracy, and free up human resources for strategic work. It refers to the use of software robots to automate highly repetitive and routine tasks that were traditionally performed by humans. It uses a set of automation tools to automate repetitive tasks and manual processes performed electronically.

To maintain competitiveness in this rapidly evolving landscape, businesses must stay abreast of technological trends and be willing to invest in RPA and related innovations. RPA can take repetitive tasks off your plate so your organization can concentrate on important, human-centric tasks. Unlike traditional automation that requires deep programming, RPA operates at the user interface level, making it easier to deploy and manage. RPA automates routine tasks, ensuring faster, more accurate, and more efficient operations. Because automation helps companies do more with less, RPA can be especially advantageous for curbing the potential effects of rising material costs, limited warehouse space, and fluctuating transportation costs. The adoption of robotic process automation is accelerating across various industries. Organizations embracing RPA understand what it really is, choose the right processes to automate, and view intelligent automation as strategic enablement.

This book examines robotic process automation (RPA) and its applications in various industries. It is organized into twelve chapters that summarize RPA and its applications in a concise manner.

Chapter 1 Introduction:

In this chapter, we will provide various applications of RPA. The chapter also serves as an introduction to the entire book. R**obotic process automation (RPA)** is a transformative automation technology that can automate business processes that are rules-based, structured, and repetitive. It uses software robots to offload routine tasks. Applications of RPA are seen in many multinational companies today. Many global corporations have already executed RPA. The RPA services provide data security, enhanced business efficiency and effectiveness across various business applications without modifying available system and infrastructure.

Chapter 2 Healthcare:

The goal of this chapter is to show how RPA is being utilized in the healthcare industry to streamline tasks, cut costs, and improve care. Robotic process automation (RPA) is a technology that has become increasingly relevant in everyday business life and has reached more and more areas, including healthcare. Healthcare organizations benefit from

RPA software through its ability to automate repetitive administrative work. RPA in healthcare uses software robots to automate repetitive tasks, reducing errors and improving efficiency. The healthcare industry has realized that automation is not a luxury; it is a survival strategy. It has finally figured out that it is cheaper, faster, and smarter to automate routine tasks and let humans do what they are best at—caring for patients.

Chapter 3 Business:

This chapter provides an overview of the benefits of RPA for businesses. Automation has changed many aspects of the business today. Robotic automation is continuing to spread into all types of businesses across the globe. Robotic process automation (RPA) involves the use of software robots or "bots" to automate repetitive, rule-based tasks that were once performed manually by employees. RPA is transforming how businesses operate. It automates repetitive business processes across a wide range of industries, including banking, accounting, IT, human resources, government, transportation, insurance, communications, and healthcare.

Chapter 4 Finance:

This chapter highlights the use of robotic process automation (RPA) in the finance industry. The main focus of RPA in finance is to replace repetitive and rule-based tasks. Software robots can do many amazing things to make the life of a finance professional much easier. RPA can help finance and accounting teams to improve efficiency, accuracy, compliance, and customer satisfaction. The emerging field of RPA in finance is proving to be a real game-changer for finance professionals. If implemented properly, RPA can prove revolutionary for the finance sector.

Chapter 5 Marketing:

This chapter investigates the adoption of RPA in marketing operations. RPA is radically transforming the marketing industry. From automated price adjustments to competitor monitoring and data management, RPA is proving to be an invaluable ally in the marketing field. By using this transformative technology, organizations can boost operational efficiency, increase accuracy, and foster innovation, setting themselves up for long-term success in a constantly evolving market. By automating repetitive tasks, RPA enables marketing teams to focus on more strategic and creative efforts. The future of RPA in marketing appears to be very promising, with many experts predicting that the technology will continue to grow and evolve in the coming years.

Chapter 6 Manufacturing:

In this chapter, we will discuss the role of RPA in the manufacturing industry. RPA executes a set of instructions to replicate tasks typically done by humans, enabling manufacturers to streamline operations, reduce costs, and minimize errors. Its impact on manufacturing is growing in several areas, including supply chain management, quality control, preventive maintenance, and administrative automation. The manufacturing industry is expected to become a huge beneficiary of RPA technology due to the manual repetitive tasks that characterize traditional aspects of manufacturing. Manufacturers are actively adopting RPA to automate voluminous and repetitive tasks that constitute their daily routines. RPA are reshaping manufacturing operations and driving unprecedented efficiency.

Chapter 7 Telecommunications:

This chapter examines the role of RPA in telecommunications. Telecom companies have been among the most active adopters of RPA. The quantity of documents they process and interactions with customers, partners, and contractors dictate the need for intelligent automation at multiple levels. Integrating RPA can help telecom companies simplify the handling of operational tasks and generate lasting revenue streams. RPA in telecom has emerged as a game-changing solution, enabling telecom companies to automate repetitive tasks, reduce operational costs, and improve service efficiency. By implementing RPA in telecom, companies can streamline their operations, improve accuracy, and free up employees to focus on more strategic tasks.

Chapter 8 Supply Chain:

In this chapter, we explore the profound effects of RPA on supply chain logistics. Supply chain automation uses RPA to make supply chain processes lean and efficient. Supply chain automation tools give companies new ways to cope with uncertainty and keep business processes and products moving. Robotics in supply chain will decrease manual labor, freeing up staff members to concentrate on more crucial tasks and lowering data analysis errors. RPA can change how we manage the supply chain. It has the potential to revolutionize supply chain management by automating repetitive tasks, improving accuracy, and driving efficiency.

Chapter 9 Logistics:

The primary goal of this chapter is to explore the potential impact of RPA on logistics processes. By automating repetitive tasks, RPA facilitates enhanced accuracy and speed, enabling companies to manage their supply chain logistics more effectively. In the logistics sector, where precision and speed are paramount, RPA has found its niche. RPA in logistics helps automate routine activities like manual data entry, shipment tracking, and delivery scheduling. As RPA tools become more prevalent, they are set to reshape the logistics and supply chain management landscape, offering new opportunities for growth and innovation.

Chapter 10 Human Resources:

This chapter emphasizes the transformative impact of robotic process automation (RPA) on human resources (HR) operations. RPA has the potential to streamline operations, enhance employee productivity, and reshape strategic HR functions. RPA in HR has streamlined operations, driven efficiency, and reduced costs in human resource operations. It helps automate a wide range of repetitive tasks and allows HR professionals to provide value-driven, human-focused work. The integration of RPA within **HR functions** offers a transformative solution to enhance operational efficiency and elevate the role of HR professionals. Robotic process automation is transforming HR operations by automating mundane tasks and enabling HR professionals to focus on strategic endeavors.

Chapter 11 Customer Service:

This chapter explores the transformative impact of robotic process automation on customer service and support teams. RPA is a breakthrough technology that is revolutionizing customer service by automating repetitive tasks, streamlining workflows, and enhancing overall efficiency. By integrating RPA into customer service (CS) workflows, businesses can enhance efficiency and allocate human agents to more complex issues, improving overall customer satisfaction, while automating customer experiences. RPA tools will play a critical role in redefining how companies approach customer service.

Chapter 12 Government:

The purpose of this chapter is to explain the adoption of robotic process automation (RPA) in the government sector. RPA is transforming government operations by streamlining time-consuming tasks and improving service delivery. It is used in government sector for several reasons, including its ability to automate mundane and repetitive tasks, reduce costs, and free up human labor for more strategic duty. RPA is the future of local government, with the power to eliminate thousands of man hours a year of manual data entry, and reduce your municipality's expenses drastically.

This is a comprehensive introductory text on the issues, ideas, theories, and applications of robotic process automation (RPA). It provides an overview of various applications in simple terms so that beginners can understand it. It is a must-read book for anyone who wants to learn RPA, which is an important emerging technology today.

I am grateful for the support of Dr. Anthony Hill, the department head of the

Department of Electrical and Computer Engineering, and Dr. Pamela Obiomon, the dean of the College of Engineering at Prairie View A&M University, Prairie View, Texas. Special thanks are due to my wife, Dr. Janet Sadiku, for helping in various ways.

M. N. O. Sadiku, Westlake, FL

Brief Table of Contents

Detailed Table of Contents

CHAPTER 1
INTRODUCTION

"He who is not courageous enough to take risks will accomplish nothing in life."
Muhammad Ali

1.1 Introduction

Busywork is not healthy for anyone, especially if you are a person who should be busy performing other, more high-priority work. Yet, for many of us, there are repetitive tasks we must complete to make it through our workday. That is why robotic process automation (RPA) is such a transformative automation technology. It uses software robots to offload routine tasks. It leverages advanced automation technology to mimic human actions and perform repetitive, rule-based tasks with speed, accuracy, and reliability. It frees us from the monotonous tasks that prevent us from getting to higher-value work [1].

The optimum way to operate a business in the modern world is robotic process automation (RPA), which brings with it the best prospects for efficiency and productivity improvements. RPA is a simple and easy-to-use automation software that deploys RPA bots that mimic human actions. RPA at its core means using software robots to automate repetitive, rule-based tasks that were before performed by human beings. It offers a chance to revolutionize the way organizations' operations are run, leading to efficiency and higher productivity levels. It can save you time and money, freeing your employees from monotonous digital tasks where human intelligence is not needed.

Robotic process automation (RPA) is a software technology that facilitates the development and management of software that simulates human actions while interfacing with digitized systems. It is transforming and revolutionizing businesses across various industries by automating low-value, mundane, time-consuming, and repetitive tasks. Applications of RPA are seen in many multinational companies today. Many global corporations have already executed RPA. The economic advantages of RPA implementation are substantial and worth emphasizing. Because RPA is great for repetitive tasks that have to follow a specific set of rules, there are multiple areas of business where these robots thrive [2].

In this chapter, we will provide various applications of RPA. The chapter serves as an introduction to the entire book. The chapter begins with introducing the concept of robotic process automation (RPA). It provides some applications of RPA. It highlights the benefits and challenges of RPA. The last section concludes with comments.

1.2 What Is Robotic Process Automation?

Among the various forms of artificial intelligence, RPA stands out for its potential to significantly increase workforce productivity by reducing or eliminating the need to do repetitive tasks manually. Popular applications of RPA include data entry, data reconciliation, spreadsheet manipulation, systems integration, automated data reporting, analytics, email notifications, acquisitions, administrative services, finance, human resources, mission assurance, strategic communications, travel reimbursements, claims processing, and customer outreach and communications. These are just a few examples of the ways RPA is being used to remove the burden of manual, repetitive, and duplicative tasks from public service workers [3].

Robotic process automation is a form of automation software. It is a technology that can automate repetitive, rules-based tasks. Like an Excel macro operating within a spreadsheet, RPA can record actions performed across a personal computer, access systems, and perform specific tasks for human users. It uses software robots, more commonly called "bots," that mimic basic human-computer interactions. 1.1 shows the symbol of RPA [4], while Figure 1.2 shows processes that RPA can automate [5]. Most industries use RPA. The government does too. Due to the repetitive nature of some tasks, the probability of human error increases. One way to eliminate errors is by using RPA.

Figure 1.1 Symbol of RPA [4].

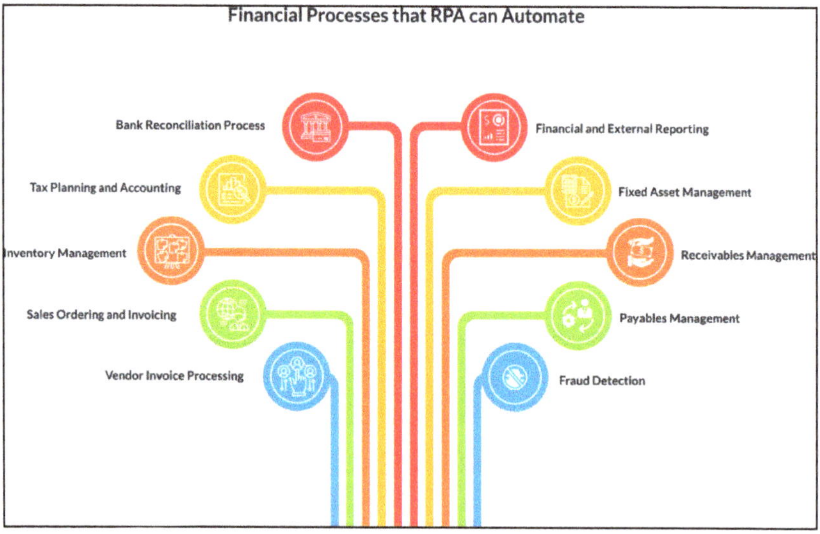

Figure 1.2 Processes that RPA can automate [5].

Robotic process automation solutions fall into three key categories: attended RPA, unattended RPA, and hybrid RPA, as shown in Figure 1.3 [6].

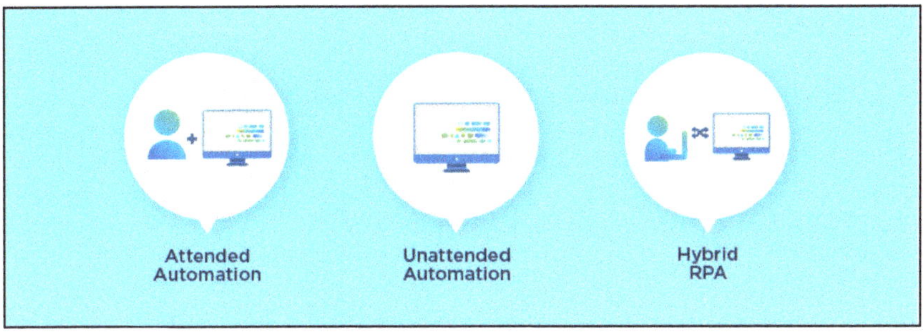

Figure 1.3 Three key categories of RPA [6].

Robotic process automation is a type of software that mimics the activity of a human being in carrying out a task within a process. It is a technology that automates repetitive tasks using software robots. RPA uses a set of automation tools to automate repetitive tasks and manual processes performed electronically. Since RPA can automate tasks that are rule-based, manual, repetitive, and tedious, delivering the highest levels of accuracy and eradicating human errors, it is a seamless fit for the finance industry. Here are some specific examples of what RPA in finance can do [7]:

- Opening emails and joining attachments
- Automatically logging into various applications on the web
- Shifting folders and files
- Copying and pasting

- Completing forms
- Collecting data from databases and the web
- Making calculations
- Connecting to system API
- Extracting structured data from documents
- Gathering stats from social media
- Following if/then decisions and rules

Some of these tasks are displayed in Figure 1.4 [6].

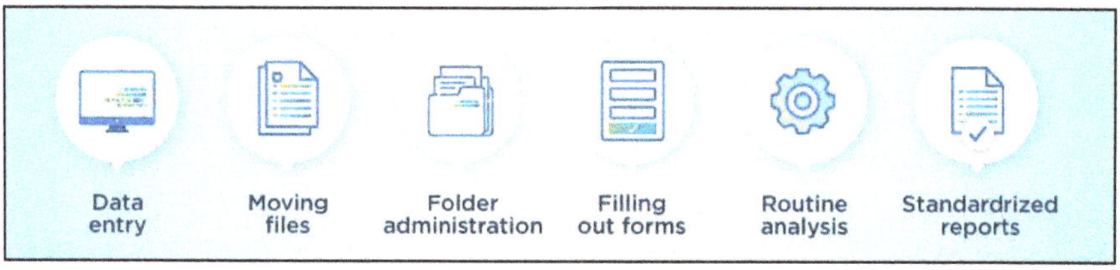

Figure 1.4 Some tasks RPA can perform [6].

At its core, robotic process automation (RPA) is a tool designed to mimic rule-based business processes, performing them seamlessly and without fatigue. RPA is a rule-driven method that is limited in its application. The technology functions much like a Microsoft Excel macro; the key difference is in power and reach. It follows set rules, similar to how an Excel macro works, to do things like move files or log into accounts. Growing as a popular solution in finance and accounting, RPA refers to software technology or "software robots" with artificial intelligence (AI) and machine learning (ML) capabilities. The "software robots" have the ability to learn and complete a high

volume of rules-based, repetitive tasks and business processes. They have the capacity to operate much faster than humans, with 100% precision and reliability, working around the clock.

Finance and human resources are just two examples of departments likely to have many use cases that RPA can help solve. Some examples of good use cases for RPA in finance include processing customer orders, ensuring timely vendor payments, and managing period-end financial close processes. For human resources, some examples include employee onboarding, time tracking, and leave of absence management. Processes where human judgment is needed are not appropriate for RPA since RPA automations rely on clear, consistently applied rules [8].

Along with RPA, one should be aware of both business process automation (BPA) and digital process automation (DPA) – two commonly used automation technologies that robotics process automation can be paired with to optimize and streamline a digital transformation. BPA refers to the use of technology to automate complex, multi-step workflows, typically very specific to a company's core business functions. DPA offers dual power by automating processes from end to end and optimizing common workflows that involve external human interactions (i.e., sales, management). Separately, RPA and AI are quite powerful, but leveraging them together is undoubtedly advantageous to any financial institution. When deployed together, AI is the "brains" behind RPA's bots [9].

1.3 Applications Of Robotic Process Automation

RPA is becoming an integral part of most modern business organizations. The numerous applications of RPA have collectively contributed to the growth of various industries. In this section, we highlight some common practical applications of robotic process automation across various industries. These include [10-14]:

- 1. *Healthcare:* Many incredibly sensitive client engagements occur in the healthcare industry, but there are also many time-consuming, tedious procedures and administrative functions that do not require technical expertise. The healthcare industry requires the services of RPA on various levels. In the healthcare sector, robotic process automation is used for automating rule-based, repetitive tasks such as patient engagement, bill payments, operational procedures, front office activities, etc. RPA reduces operational costs, streamlines activities, and speeds up processes. It can cut costs, enhance the pace of procedures, maximize the productivity of business processes, and optimize the patients' experiences in healthcare institutions. Figure 1.5 shows RPA in healthcare [15].

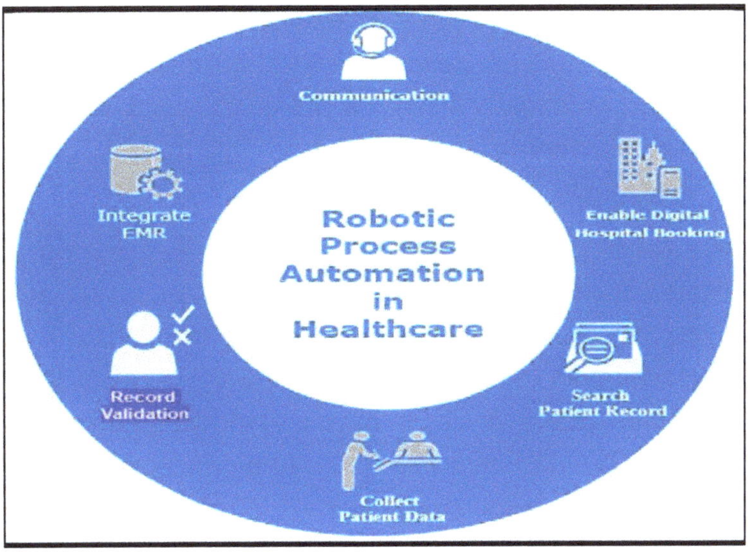

Figure 1.5 RPA in healthcare [15].

- 2. *Manufacturing:* In manufacturing industries, robotic process automation is used to automate tasks like order processing, inventory management, quality control, etc. Automating these mundane tasks, it helps improve consistency and efficiency in production. It also allows organizations to reduce production time and errors, which in turn reduces the production costs.
- 3. *Business:* RPA is a type of business automation that automates digital tasks that are high-volume, repetitive, and rule-based. Observing the rapid expansion and the rate at which firms across industries have implemented RPA, it is apparent that RPA is forming the underpinning for modern business operations in the digital world. The applications of RPA are expanding at an exponential rate, and businesses that do not adopt RPA and automation technologies are likely to fall behind since they would not be able to compete on an equal

footing. RPA has the power to revolutionize workplace productivity and efficiency. Thanks to automation, data transfers, order processing, and payroll calculations are just some of the repeatable tasks business departments no longer have to worry about.

- 4. *Supply Chain:* Many of the tasks, processes, and workflows that form crucial links in the supply chain can be enhanced by RPA. Process automation can be a key component of any organization's supply chain optimization initiatives. RPA in supply chain is expected to have a significant influence on the business process industry in areas of production, efficiency, and precision. In the supply chain, RPA is employed to automate processes that are now performed manually, leaving minimal possibility for errors and aberrations. Instead of monotonous, tedious tasks, companies will be able to recruit and educate employees for problem-solving and brainstorming assignments, leveraging robots.
- 5. *Finance:* Finance functions tend to have strict rules and frameworks governing their operations. Across accounts payable, accounts receivable, and beyond, many financial processes involve highly repetitive data entry or calculations. RPA excels at automating routine tasks, including account reconciliation and invoice processing.
- 6. *Banking*: The banking industry involves multiple repetitive tasks, all prioritizing data accuracy. RPA is used in the banking sector for automating tasks that consume much time, like loan processing, account reconciliation, compliance checks, etc. It minimizes dependency on human employees for repetitive operations. Applying RPA frees up time for employees to focus on other cardinal areas of the company. RPA assists banking and accounting departments in

automating time-consuming manual operations, allowing employees to focus on more important activities and gain a strategic edge for the company. RPA has been widely utilized in the industry to help organize and automate time-consuming banking activities.

- 7. *Accounting:* Accounting is an essential function in any business, as it is the backbone that records financial transactions and maintains information for tax purposes. Faced with shifts in client expectations and a revolving door of regulatory changes, more and more accounting companies are turning to technology to automate workflows and improve operational efficiencies. It is no secret that accounting companies are increasingly looking for ways to improve efficiencies and drive greater profitability. With the rise of technology, accounting work can be done more efficiently by robotic process automation software. RPA is a great way to automate repetitive, mundane tasks in bookkeeping, invoicing, tax compliance, accounts payable or receivable, payroll, expense management, and more. This eases the strain on staff and provides them with more time to focus on higher-value, higher-margin work.
- 8. *Customer Service:* The biggest challenge in the customer service industry is for employees to remember their customers' entire personal or billing history. Researching every customer manually is a tiresome activity. RPA software can automate difficult tasks like going through customer history and, thus, save time and money. It improves and enhances customer service by reducing administrative workload. Customer service is sped up with software robots that gather data and documents from various systems, handle service requests, and update customer records.

- 9. *Human Resources*: RPA is gaining traction among human resources (HR) professionals as additional use cases emerge. The HR department deals with the most cumbersome tasks like employee onboarding, data management, etc. HR managers are tasked with payroll, applicant sourcing, travel, exit management, and more. Automation of just one of these tasks can save a ton of time and money. RPA is currently often used in HR to automate tasks, including consolidating or reviewing datasets, issuing job offer letters to candidates, onboarding new hires, enabling health plan registration, and even making badges for conferences and special events. Using RPA in HR opens a lot of opportunities for professionals to focus on other areas, and they can focus on the current employee performance while recruiting new ones. Figure 1.6 shows the role of RPA in human resources [12].

Figure 1.6 Role of RPA in human resources [12].

- 10. *Insurance:* In the insurance industry, companies are battling legacy systems, siloed functions and teams, complex operating structures, limited underwriting talent, and the constant need to deliver a great customer experience across insurance claims and underwriting processes. RPA helps insurance companies win those battles through the automation of repetitive tasks that take up too much valuable employee time.
- 11. *Public Sector*: The public sector is essential for the well-being of the public. That means it needs to run efficiently so that people can get the help and support they need from the government. The challenge is that companies in this industry are always short on time and short on budget. Automation can help give them both back, at least in part. RPA helps the public sector to enable better care of the public and their workforce through data capture and analysis (surveys and census management).

Some applications of RPA are displayed in Figure 1.7 [16].

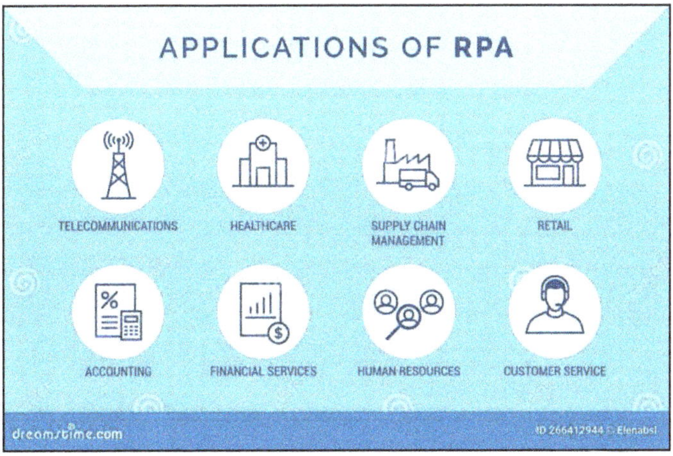

Figure 1.7 Some applications of RPA [16].

1.4 Benefits

Implementing RPA helps streamline repetitive tasks, maximize productivity, and increase efficiency. The principal advantage of automation with RPA is that you are taking the burden of repetitive tasks off the shoulders of your staff, thereby freeing them up to focus on more complicated workflows while bots handle repetitive high-volume tasks. RPA reduces labor costs as well as prevents human error. Other benefits include the following [13,17,18]:

- *Cost Savings*: By automating manual processes and optimizing resource utilization, RPA helps businesses reduce operational costs associated with labor, inventory management, and production inefficiencies. The cost savings derived from RPA implementation can be reinvested in research and development initiatives or allocated to strategic growth initiatives.
- *Eliminating Human Error*: Realistically, no matter how skilled a person is in their role, human error and fatigue are always factors to be considered. With RPA, automated bots never get tired, so tasks are performed accurately each time.
- *Increasing Compliance*: Compliance is important for the reliability and sustainability of your business, and RPA solutions adhere to set rules and guidelines with great accuracy and consistency. Typically, most organizations follow various industry and government regulations, and these organizations reap the benefits of RPA with automated, consistent compliance.
- *Boosts Efficiency:* RPA is a key catalyst for enhanced business productivity. RPA can significantly impact process

efficiency, resulting in time and cost savings, productivity boosts, and operational flexibility. Automation of mundane everyday tasks frees up time for employees, which can be directed to producing useful results. A combination of the work done by RPA and the employees shows a spike in productivity. This results in an overall increase in company efficiency and savings.

- *Improves Data Security:* Data leaks or breaches are an eternal concern for business owners and employees. It jeopardizes the integrity of the company and its employees. Programming RPA with the right parameters helps in maximizing security and reducing the chances of a data breach. By reducing the rate of human involvement in guarding said data, you are increasing its security.
- *Better Decision-making:* Analytics on overall company performance is essential to decide the future course of the company and its work methods. Applications of RPA in organizations help in data collection and decision-making. Decision-making becomes easier when it helps you identify, categorize, and retrieve information at any point.
- *Better Communication:* Updating every little detail on your systems on a daily basis can get redundant. Automating such processes helps keep every team member, manager, stakeholder, etc., in the loop. Communication is easier with RPA, and RPA results in updated employees and an efficient workforce by streamlining repetitive tasks.
- *Data Storage*: Big data is a huge aspect of modern business. Businesses possess more data now than ever before, and the volume of data is growing exponentially. Effectively sorting through your mountains of data is vital. RPA is invaluable to

organizations because it can sift through large amounts of data tirelessly, with no errors, 24/7. Robotic process automation can monitor, collect, and store relevant data, flagging any concerns that the IT needs to investigate along the way.

- *Data Analytics:* Removing the human element from data gathering is also important when it comes to providing you with data analytics and insights. The amount of data in business provides great opportunities for valuable insights into what can be improved within your processes. For decision-makers, quality data is crucial. With RPA solutions in place, the accuracy and quality of data are much higher than when processed manually.

Some benefits of RPA are depicted in Figure 1.8 [12].

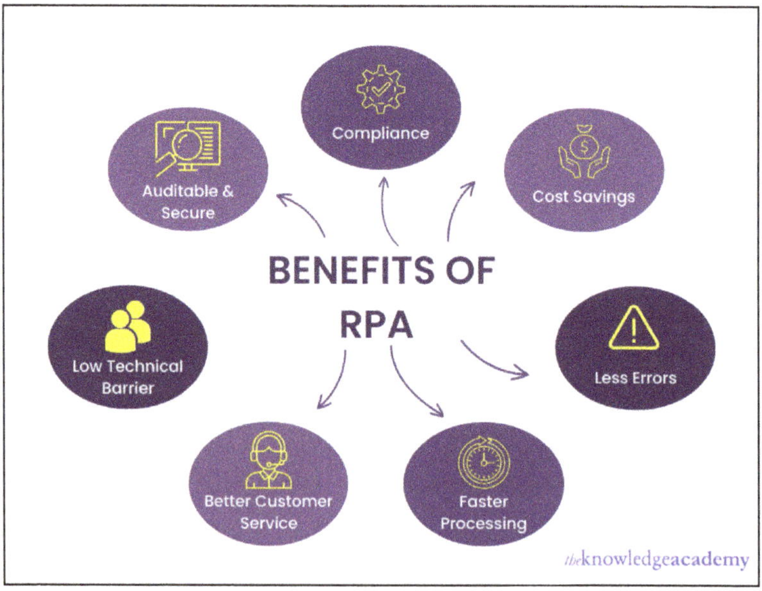

Figure 1.8 Some benefits of RPA [12].

1.5 Challenges

Robotic process automation challenges have emerged as critical considerations in the modern business landscape, where the promise of streamlined processes clashes with the complexities of implementation. Implementation of RPA usually faces different challenges that touch on technology, organizational, and process areas. The most common RPA challenges organizations meet fall into three categories: technical, business, and regulatory. Thus, the key challenges include the following [19,20]:

- *Technical Challenges*: One of the first challenges businesses must consider when planning RPA implementation is compatibility with the currently used software. A company's existing systems often combine different technologies, user interfaces, and protocols that need to stay in sync. RPA works best with structured data and may require additional technologies like AI or OCR (optical character recognition) to process unstructured datasets.
- *Business Challenges*: New technologies give rise to new possibilities but also new challenges. If you ignore the people relevant to the automated processes, you will likely face fear or even outright aversion to the new technology. Usually, any change to the tried and true ways of doing things is met with strong resistance from employees, even if the change will eventually be for the better. Treating RPA implementation as an opportunity to revisit your current operations is essential.
- *Regulatory Challenges*: Legal requirements pose another major challenge for organizations considering RPA.

Depending on the automated process, bots may process sensitive data such as customer records, financial data, and personal information that you are legally obligated to keep secure. You must establish RPA governance rules defining responsibilities and ownership at all automation and data processing stages. RPA implementation adds another potential surface for cyber threats.

- *Ethical Concerns:* With technological developments and ethical concerns influencing how RPA has evolved, businesses need to be adaptable to follow trends while observing ethical practices as well as human-friendly principles.
- *Integration Complexity:* The most common robotic process automation challenge is integration complexity, as RPA systems often struggle to seamlessly connect with legacy systems, diverse software applications, and evolving IT infrastructures, requiring extensive customization, technical expertise, and ongoing maintenance to ensure smooth and efficient automation workflows. The complexity arises from the need to ensure that RPA technology operates harmoniously alongside existing software applications and legacy systems.
- *Implementation Costs:* The implementation involves not only the acquisition of the solution itself but also the costs associated with customization, training, and system integration. These upfront financial commitments can present a significant challenge, especially for smaller enterprises with limited budgets.
- *Change Resistance:* Change management resistance emerges as a critical challenge when organizations embark on the adoption of robotic process automation. The introduction of automated

processes often triggers resistance among employees accustomed to traditional workflows. Employees may perceive RPA as a threat to job security or may resist the need to adapt to new technologies. Communication, education, and involving employees in the transition process are essential elements in mitigating resistance.

- *Scalability*: This is important when planning to scale up RPA initiatives across organizations, as this requires careful resource allocation and planning to ensure it happens optimally. One of the main limitations of robotic process automation is limited scalability, as it struggles with complex, non-routine tasks. Overcoming the limitations of scalability requires a strategic approach, including selecting flexible tools, designing processes with future scalability in mind, and continuously reassessing automation strategies to align with the evolving demands of the business landscape.
- *Lack of Skilled Talent:* The shortage of skilled talent in designing, implementing, and maintaining RPA systems creates a significant bottleneck. This scarcity negatively affects the seamless integration and optimization of automation initiatives within organizations. Companies aiming to leverage it must navigate the competitive landscape for skilled professionals, invest in training programs, and foster a culture that attracts and retains individuals with the necessary expertise.

Some challenges s of RPA are depicted in Figure 1.9 [20].

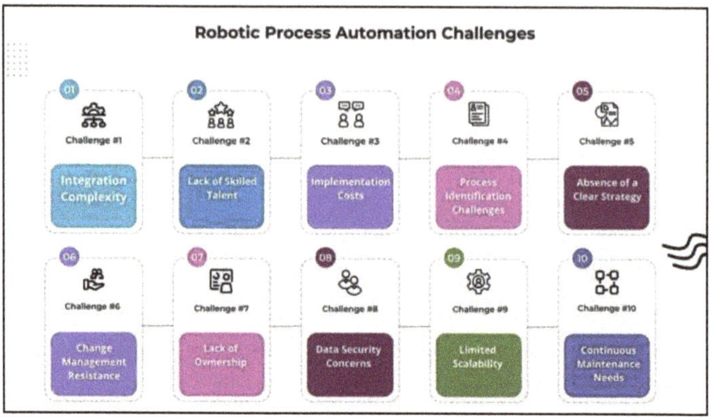

Figure 1.9 Some challenges of RPA [20].

1.6 Conclusion

RPA is a technology that can automate business processes that are rules-based, structured, and repetitive. It stands for virtual or invisible robots, which sit inside the systems, moving between various applications, checking, inputting, updating, and processing more promptly than a human could. This type of automation employs software bots to execute large volumes of tasks in business processes, freeing up human resources to focus on more complex tasks. The RPA services provide data security, enhanced business efficiency, and effectiveness across various business applications without modifying the available system and infrastructure. The applications of RPA across various industries have significantly contributed to their growth. RPA will soon achieve near-universal acceptance if its astronomic growth continues. More information about the applications of robotic process automation can be found in the books [21-27].

References

[1] "Four surprising ways to automate daily work tasks with Robotic Process Automation (RPA),"

https://www.ibm.com/think/topics/rpa-use-cases

[2] M. N. O. Sadiku and J. O. Sadiku, "Applications of robotic process automation," *International Journal of Trend in Research and Development*, vol. 13, no. 1, January-February 2026, pp. 116-121.

[3] N. Komitsky, "Putting robotic process automation to work in the federal government,"

https://www.managementconcepts.com/resource/putting-robotic-process-automation-to-work-in-the-federal-government/

[4] "What is robotic process automation (RPA)? How does it work?" February 2023,

https://solidpro-es.com/what-is-robotic-process-automation-rpa-how-it-works/

[5] F. Caltin, "RPA in finance," February 2020,

https://www.plutushealthinc.com/post/rpa-in-finance

[6] "Absolutely everything you need to know about robotic process automation,"

https://www.blueprism.com/guides/robotic-process-automation-rpa/

[7] S. Donnelly, "5 Benefits of robotic process automation in finance," September 2022,

https://www.financealliance.io/5-benefits-of-robotic-process-automation-in-finance/

[8] "Robotic process automation in finance," September 2023,

https://kmbs.konicaminolta.us/blog/robotic-process-automation-in-finance/

[9] "Robotic process automation in finance,"

https://planergy.com/blog/robotic-process-automation-finance/

[10] "Applications of robotic process automation," July 2022,

https://intone.com/top-applications-of-robotic-process-automation/

[11] "Applications of robotic process automation,"

https://www.tutorialspoint.com/robotic-process-automation/robotic-process-automation-applications.htm

[12] L. Turner, "Top 5 applications of RPA - Benefits & use cases," October 2025,

https://www.theknowledgeacademy.com/blog/top-applications-of-rpa/

[13] "Chapter 4: Top robotic process automation (RPA) use cases,"

https://www.blueprism.com/automation-journey/robotic-process-automation-rpa-use-cases/

[14] "What accountants need to know about robotic process automation,"

https://tax.thomsonreuters.com/en/insights/articles/what-accountants-should-know-about-robotic-process-automation

[15] https://www.researchgate.net/figure/llustrates-the-application-of-RPA-with-AI-stages-in-healthcare_fig4_380877060

[16] https://www.dreamstime.com/rpa-robotic-process-automation-application-areas-icons-set-robotic-process-automation-applications-icons-image266412944

[17] "7 Use cases for robotic process automation (RPA)," April 2025,

https://www.impactmybiz.com/blog/blog-7-uses-robotic-process-automation-rpa/

[18] "What you should know about the benefits of RPA,"

https://www.microsoft.com/en-us/power-platform/products/power-automate/topics/robotic-process-automation/benefits-of-rpa-robotic-process-automation

[19] "Top 10 RPA implementation challenges to be aware of," August 2023,

https://flobotics.io/blog/rpa-challenges/

[20] "11 Robotic process automation challenges to overcome," February 2025,

https://theecmconsultant.com/robotic-process-automation-challenges/#google_vignette

[21] C. Juarez, *Unleashing Efficiency: The Power of Robotic Process Automation (RPA).* Independently Published, 2023.

[22] H. Mahey, *Robotic Process Automation with Automation Anywhere: Techniques to Fuel Business Productivity And Intelligent Automation Using RPA.* Packt Publishing, 2020.

[24] T. Taulli, *The Robotic Process Automation Handbook: A Guide to Implementing RPA Systems.* Apress, 2020.

[25] R. Murdoch, *Robotic Process Automation: Guide To Building Software Robots, Automate Repetitive Tasks & Become An RPA Consultant.* Independently published, 2018.

[26] C. Czarnecki and P. Fettke (eds.), *Robotic Process Automation: Management, Technology, Applications.* De Gruyter, 2021.

[27] R. Kumar, *Robotic Process Automation (RPA) and Its Applications.* Admit Hub Ref Service Press, 2024.

CHAPTER 2
ROBOTIC PROCESS AUTOMATION IN HEALTHCARE

"Educating the mind without educating the heart is no education at all."
Aristotle

2.1 Introduction

The evolution of technology has provided the business world with substantial improvements in the execution of its activities. Robotic process automation (RPA) is a technology that has become increasingly relevant in everyday business life and has reached more and more areas, including healthcare. RPA software uses "robots" (or simply "bots") to perform many of an organization's repetitive, high-volume tasks without needing human intervention. An RPA robot tends to do as it is told. It completes specific assignments according to specific parameters. It is capable of completing large volumes of work in a fraction of the time taken by human employees. With RPA robots, the potential for human error is lessened. These bots do the same tasks that humans do, but with more speed and no mistakes. Healthcare organizations benefit from RPA software through its ability to automate repetitive administrative work. RPA in healthcare uses software robots to automate repetitive tasks, reducing errors and improving efficiency. Figure 2.1 defines robotic process automation [1], while Figure 2.2 shows some healthcare professionals [2].

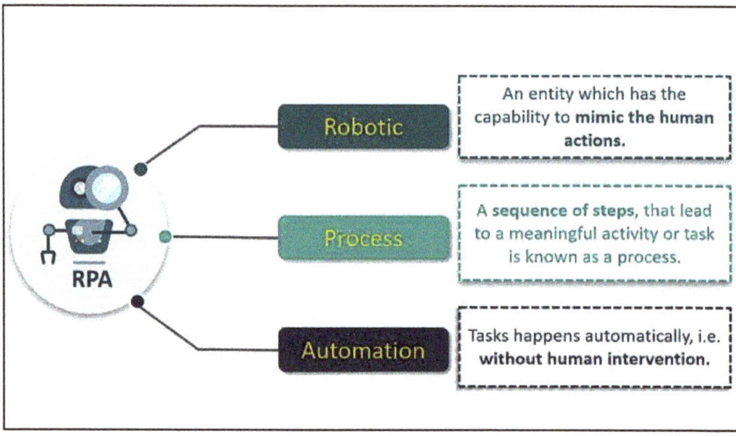

Figure 2.1 A definition of robotic process automation [1].

Figure 2.2 Some healthcare professionals [2].

Robotic process automation (RPA) involves using software robots to mimic time-consuming and repetitive processes in healthcare operations. It is a smart tool used in healthcare. It refers to the use of software robots or "bots" to automate repetitive, rule-based tasks and processes, allowing healthcare organizations to streamline their operations and improve efficiency. RPA bots manage patient data, carry out manual tasks, and give error-free answers. With less time spent on boring, time-consuming, repetitive tasks, medical staff have more time for important duties like looking after patients [3].

The goal of this chapter is to show how RPA is being utilized in the healthcare industry to streamline tasks, cut costs, and improve care. The chapter begins with introducing the concept of robotic process automation (RPA). It describes RPA in healthcare and provides some of its applications. It highlights the benefits and challenges of RPA in healthcare. It predicts the future of RPA in healthcare. The last section concludes with comments.

2.2 What Is Robotic Process Automation?

Among the various forms of artificial intelligence, RPA stands out for its potential to significantly increase workforce productivity by reducing or eliminating the need to do repetitive tasks manually. Popular applications of RPA include data entry, data reconciliation, spreadsheet manipulation, systems integration, automated data reporting, analytics, email notifications, acquisitions, administrative services, finance, human resources, mission assurance, strategic communications, travel reimbursements, claims processing, and customer outreach and communications. These are just a few examples of the ways RPA is being used to remove the burden of manual, repetitive, and duplicative tasks from public service workers [4].

Robotic process automation is a form of automation software. It is a technology that can automate repetitive, rules-based tasks. Like an Excel macro operating within a spreadsheet, RPA can record actions performed across a personal computer, access systems, and perform specific tasks for human users. It uses software robots, more commonly called "bots," that mimic basic human-computer interactions. Figure 2.3 shows the symbol of RPA [5], while Figure 2.4 shows processes that RPA can automate [6]. Most industries use RPA. The government does too. Due to the repetitive nature of some tasks, the probability of human error increases. One way to eliminate errors is by using RPA.

Figure 2.3 Symbol of RPA [5].

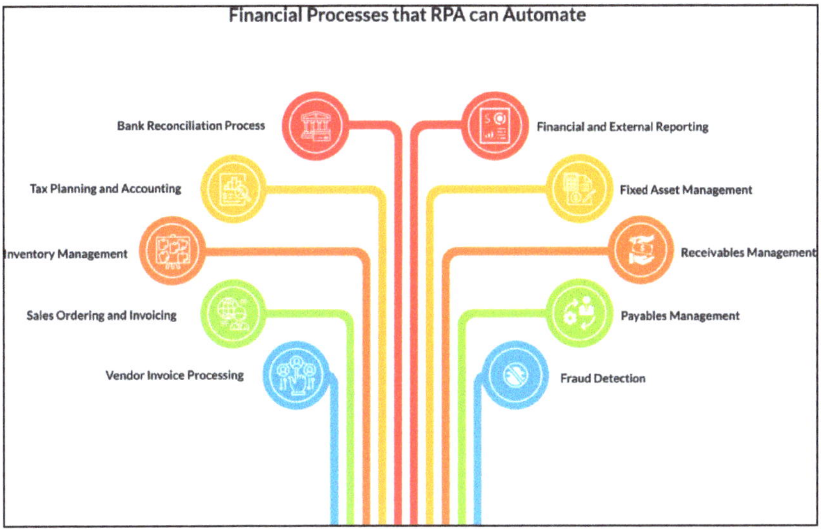

Figure 2.4 Processes that RPA can automate [6].

Robotic process automation solutions fall into three key categories: attended RPA, unattended RPA, and hybrid RPA, as shown in Figure 2.5 [7].

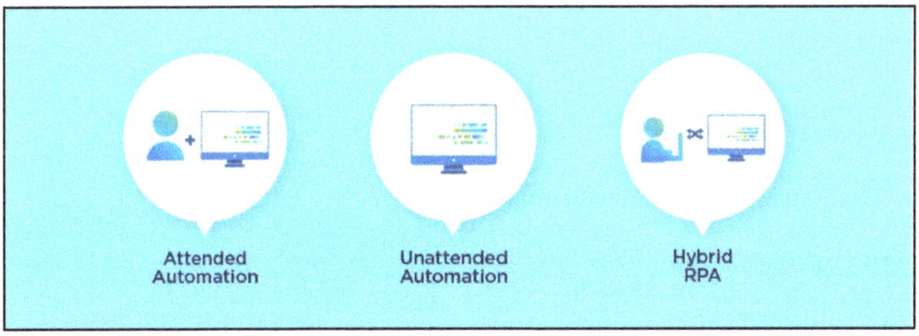

Figure 2.5 Three key categories of RPA [7].

Robotic process automation is a type of software that mimics the activity of a human being in carrying out a task within a process. It is a technology that automates repetitive tasks using software robots. RPA uses a set of automation tools to automate repetitive tasks and manual processes performed electronically. Since RPA can automate tasks that are rule-based, manual, repetitive, and tedious, delivering the highest levels of accuracy and eradicating human errors, it is a seamless fit for the finance industry. Here are some specific examples of what RPA in finance can do [8]:

- Opening emails and joining attachments
- Automatically logging into various applications on the web
- Shifting folders and files
- Copying and pasting
- Completing forms
- Collecting data from databases and the web
- Making calculations
- Connecting to system API
- Extracting structured data from documents
- Gathering stats from social media
- Following if/then decisions and rules

Some of these tasks are displayed in Figure 2.6 [7].

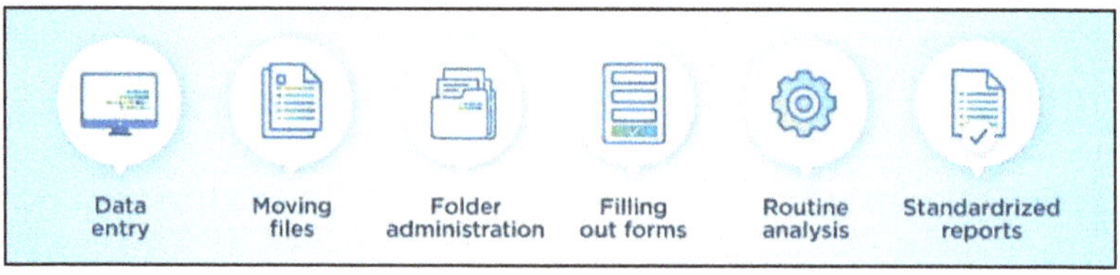

Figure 2.6 Some tasks RPA can perform [6].

At its core, robotic process automation (RPA) is a tool designed to mimic rule-based business processes, performing them seamlessly and without fatigue. RPA is a rule-driven method that is limited in its application. The technology functions much like a Microsoft Excel macro; the key difference is in power and reach. It follows set rules, similar to how an Excel macro works, to do things like move files or log into accounts. Growing as a popular solution in finance and accounting, RPA refers to software technology or "software robots" with artificial intelligence (AI) and machine learning (ML) capabilities. The "software robots" have the ability to learn and complete a high volume of rules-based, repetitive tasks and business processes. They have the capacity to operate much faster than humans, with 100% precision and reliability, working around the clock.

Finance and human resources are just two examples of departments likely to have many use cases that RPA can help solve. Some examples of good use cases for RPA in finance include processing customer orders, ensuring timely vendor payments, and managing period-end financial close processes. For human resources, some examples include employee onboarding, time tracking, and leave of absence management. Processes where human judgment is needed are not appropriate for RPA since RPA automations rely on clear, consistently applied rules [9].

Along with RPA, one should be aware of both business process automation (BPA) and digital process automation (DPA) – two commonly used automation technologies that robotics process automation can be paired with to optimize and streamline a digital transformation. BPA refers to the use of technology to automate complex, multi-step workflows, typically very specific to a company's core business functions. DPA offers dual power by automating processes from end to end and optimizing common workflows that involve external human interactions (i.e., sales, management). Separately, RPA and AI are quite powerful, but leveraging them together is undoubtedly advantageous to any financial institution. When deployed together, AI is the "brains" behind RPA's bots [10].

2.3 Robotic Process Automation In Healthcare

The healthcare industry in any country is one of the largest sectors when it comes to revenue generation and employment. It comprises medical devices, clinical trials, health insurance, and medical equipment, etc. Today, the healthcare industry is overburdened by high costs, incredibly high volume, and stringent regulations. These pressures can challenge the quality and urgency of patient care. Cumbersome, error-prone tasks slow down processes and affect everything from cost structures to compliance to the patient experience. The healthcare industry involves many highly sensitive interactions with customers, but it also includes many time-consuming, repetitive tasks and administrative tasks that do not require specialized knowledge. Robotic process automation (RPA) can provide task automation across the organization.

RPA is an automation technology that uses software to mimic the back-office tasks of human workers, such as extracting data, filling in forms, and moving files. The power of RPA in healthcare is immense. RPA in healthcare refers to the use of software robots or “bots” to automate repetitive tasks and processes in healthcare settings, such as data entry, appointment scheduling, and claims processing.

With the pressure to reduce costs, increase the speed of operations, simplify tasks, increase the efficiency of business processes, and improve the patient experience, healthcare organizations are positioned to benefit greatly from RPA. By automating repetitive tasks and managing patient data, RPA can improve efficiency, reduce costs, and enhance the overall quality of care. RPA software creates efficiencies by automating tasks that improve the accuracy of data and reporting and enable decisions to be made more quickly [11].

RPA is not a hammer for every nail. When applied strategically, it transforms outcomes. When misapplied, it just adds technical debt. Successful implementations hinge on governance, orchestration, and frontline buy-in. To successfully implement robotic process automation (RPA) in healthcare, it is important to choose the right tasks for automation. For the process to be automated, it should involve repetitive tasks.

It is also important to take an iterative approach, which requires implementing RPA in stages or steps instead of trying to automate everything at once. The implementation of robotic process automation in healthcare presents multiple opportunities to decrease expenses while reducing time requirements and enhancing medical care delivery.

2.4 Applications Of Robotic Process Automation In Healthcare

RPA use cases are plentiful in number. You can look to implement automation anywhere your organization has rules-based processes. RPA can be applied in various areas of healthcare, such as automating tasks, appointment scheduling, electronic medical records and data sharing, revenue cycle management, claims processing, HR management, medical billing, and research data reporting. RPA demonstrates its value through these applications by enhancing precision and decreasing human work while speeding up service delivery. Common areas of application of RPA in healthcare include the following [11-13]:

- *Automation:* Automation of tasks can save a lot of time and money. It streamlines processes and reduces the time and effort required for manual file transfers. Automation of processes has been very successful in the healthcare sector when the goals are well laid down, and the planning is done well. Automation tools like RPA can contribute to reduced wait times and increased efficiency, allowing patients to receive faster and more efficient care. By automating processes, RPA ensures that tasks are performed consistently and accurately, reducing the risk of errors or non-compliance and worker burnout. By automating administrative tasks through RPA, healthcare organizations can reduce the burden on their staff members and create a better work-life balance. For example, file movement automation is one of the potential use cases of robotic process automation (RPA) in healthcare. It involves automating the process of transferring files between different systems and platforms used in healthcare settings. File movement automation saves time, improves efficiency in healthcare operations, enhances data management, and facilitates seamless file movement throughout the organization. In healthcare, RPA can be used to automate communications like responses to inquiries on the website, first-line calls to customer service, front-line administrator queries, and email blasts to patients, vendors, and staff.

- *Appointment Scheduling:* Patient scheduling benefits from automation, particularly in large healthcare networks where appointment management is complex. RPA is a great tool for appointment scheduling. It can take care of most tasks in this area. From setting up the meeting based on the doctor's availability to confirming patient schedules, no job is too big or small. This technology also sends reminders so no one forgets their visit. Appointment scheduling bots can manage cancellations, rescheduling, and waitlist notifications, improving utilization and patient satisfaction. RPA is used to track and request approval for patients as appointments are made, attended, or canceled. Using RPA leads to fewer errors and saves staff time.
- *Electronic Medical Records:* The healthcare industry is highly regulated, requiring very stringent protocols and reporting with respect to patient records, medical records, and other sensitive information. Electronic medical records (EMRs) and data sharing are essential elements in healthcare. With the help of robotic process automation (RPA), these processes can be

streamlined and made more efficient. RPA can automate tasks like updating EMRs. By reducing human error and improving accuracy, RPA improves the quality, completeness, timeliness, and interoperability of healthcare data. RPA bots can be integrated into a hospital's electronic health record (EHR) system to extract patient data from intake forms, verify insurance eligibility in real time, and flag inconsistencies for human review. This approach allows organizations to eliminate manual steps and reduce processing time.

- *Medical Billing:* Healthcare providers handle numerous bills and payments on a daily basis, including those for doctor visits, tests, medicines, and hospital stays. RPA bots and agentic automation solutions can be used to streamline the settlement of health payments, expediting claims processing, minimizing billing errors and disputes, and ensuring transparency across financial operations.
- *Research Reporting:* Research data reporting is a potential use case of robotic process automation (RPA) in the healthcare industry. RPA can automate the process of collecting and analyzing research data, making it more efficient and accurate. With RPA, healthcare organizations can streamline their data reporting workflows, saving time and resources. By automating research data reporting, healthcare providers can focus on interpreting results and making informed decisions based on the collected information.
- *Data Entry:* In healthcare organizations, many repetitive processes and decisions rely on the availability of accurate data. Administrative data is just one of many types of data encountered in a healthcare setting. Administrative data entry often does not require specialized skills, but it is a task that can be very repetitive. RPA can be used to take data inputs

from various sources, some of which may need to be converted to structured data using bots. That data must then be input into a database or other repository for use by the organization. RPA boosts data accuracy and safety. Bots move and enter data with fewer mistakes. They enhance data entry processes by eliminating errors and facilitating interoperability across multiple healthcare systems.

- *Data Management:* RPA in healthcare involves using software solutions to automate repetitive tasks, like patient data management. Modern automation solutions can assist with patient data management. RPA tools automatically collect, verify, and update patient data across disparate systems. This ensures real-time accuracy, improves access to critical information, and reduces the likelihood of documentation errors. Automation also streamlines workflows related to medical records, reducing time spent on repetitive data entry while ensuring data integrity across healthcare platforms. Healthcare RPA software ensures that data is consistently accurate and up-to-date. RPA bots can also log into government healthcare scheme portals, capture patient transaction records, and verify their statuses. Upon successful data validation, the robot automatically informs relevant departments via email. RPA can analyze data from various sources, identify patterns of non-compliance, and trigger alerts for corrective actions.
- *HR Management:* Due to the continuous personnel shortage in the healthcare sector, efficient management of the existing health workforce has become critical to organizations' performance. Staffing optimization is one of the potential use cases of robotic process automation (RPA) in healthcare. By introducing RPA, healthcare organizations can improve efficiency and reduce costs related to workforce management.

With RPA, tasks such as staff scheduling and resource allocation can be automated, saving time and ensuring optimal staffing levels. Healthcare organizations can enhance human resource (HR) management by adopting agentic and robotic process automation.

- *Insurance Authorization:* Sometimes, healthcare providers are required to undergo a prior authorization process so that a patient's insurance provider covers certain prescribed medications or medical procedures, which can be time-consuming, especially when done on a large scale. Automating insurance verification, medical necessity checks, and documentation submission significantly reduces approval times. A major advantage of RPA is streamlining billing and claims processing. RPA automates insurance verification, cross-checks patient information, and flags errors before claims are submitted, reducing rejections. Obtaining prior authorization from payers often involves repetitive retrieval of clinical documents, form-filling, and status tracking. RPA and AI technology are used to submit and follow up on requests for prior authorization for procedures, communicating automatically with the patient and all involved constituents, and often scheduling the procedure. Since insurance authorization submissions are dependent upon proper coding, AI technology can identify and sometimes resolve inconsistencies in submissions caused by manual errors.
- *Pharmacy Operations:* Pharmacy operations are another area where RPA is making strides, particularly in medication inventory management. Automated tracking systems monitor stock levels, predict demand trends, and flag potential shortages before they impact patient care. Automated prescription verification also ensures compliance with safety protocols, reducing dispensing errors.

- *Predictive Analytics:* An emerging trend is the use of RPA in predictive analytics for operational efficiency and patient management. By analyzing historical data, automated systems can forecast patient admission rates, optimize staffing schedules, and anticipate supply chain needs. Hospitals utilizing predictive automation have reported reductions in emergency department overcrowding through early detection of patient surges.

2.5 Benefits

While performing discrete, specific tasks, RPA services provide a range of important benefits. These include lower administrative costs, enhanced data security, improved efficiency, increased accuracy, improved compliance, improved patient experience, reduction of burnout, improved clinical outcomes, and scalability. RPA technology can have a significant impact on an organization's productivity, efficiency, cash flow, and revenue. Other benefits include the following [11,12,14]:

- *Cost Reduction:* Automation reduces the labor hours needed to perform routine tasks. Implementing robotic process automation (RPA) in healthcare can lead to lower administrative costs. By automating repetitive and time-consuming tasks, such as appointment scheduling, revenue cycle management, and claims processing, healthcare organizations can save money on staffing and streamline their operations. This cost reduction makes RPA services for the healthcare industry an attractive investment for long-term financial sustainability.

- *Error Reduction:* By eliminating manual data entry, RPA reduces the likelihood of billing errors or documentation mistakes. This is vital in healthcare, where small inaccuracies can result in denied claims or compromised care quality.
- *Customer Service:* RPA bots can be used to automate repetitive customer service and remote care activities, providing the ability to address repetitive questions with consistency and expediency. RPA can also be used in follow-up for remote care, following business rules to deliver specific communication at certain steps in the patient care plan. It improves the patient experience with more consistent care because of more accurate decisions, reduced costs, and greater visibility across the entire patient record.
- *Reducing Human Errors:* RPA helps reduce human error, resulting in fewer costly mistakes and improved efficiency in handling administrative tasks. RPA offers a cost-effective solution for improving operational effectiveness in the healthcare industry. It improves the accuracy of data, tasks, and reporting in clinical settings and others by reducing human error, ensuring task and output consistency, and enabling organizations to successfully put best practices in place.
- *Enhanced Data Security*: RPA in healthcare can significantly enhance data security by implementing various measures to protect sensitive information. This includes encryption, which helps to secure data by converting it into a code that can only be accessed with the correct decryption key. Access controls are also implemented, ensuring that only authorized individuals have permission to view or modify certain data. By prioritizing privacy measures, risk management, and compliance regulations, RPA ensures that healthcare

institutions can maintain secure systems and protect patient information from potential threats.

- *Improved Efficiency:* RPA in healthcare can greatly improve efficiency across various processes. By automating repetitive and time-consuming tasks, RPA technology enables streamlined operations and enhanced performance. Adopting RPA in healthcare enhances operational efficiency, allowing staff to focus on more critical aspects of patient care.
- *Increased Accuracy:* Robotic process automation (RPA) can greatly increase accuracy in healthcare processes. By automating tasks such as data entry and record management, RPA reduces the chances of human error. This leads to enhanced precision, improved data integrity, and reliable processing of medical information.
- *Reduction of Burnout:* Healthcare professionals often experience burnout due to the overwhelming amount of paperwork and data handling they are responsible for. Robotic process automation (RPA) can help alleviate burnout among healthcare workers by minimizing their administrative tasks. By implementing RPA, the manual tasks can be automated, allowing healthcare workers to focus more on patient care and reducing the risk of burnout.
- *Scalability:* Robotic process automation in healthcare bots can be scaled up or down to match demand, such as seasonal spikes in appointments or periodic regulatory reporting. The scalability of robotic process automation (RPA) in healthcare is a key benefit that allows for the automation of high-volume, rule-based, and repetitive tasks. RPA tools can handle large amounts of data and tasks efficiently, making it easier to manage administrative workflows. This scalability

ensures that healthcare organizations can streamline their processes and optimize operations.

- *Regulatory Compliance:* Regulatory compliance is dependent upon accuracy, consistency, and protection of records, which RPA can provide. Automation ensures that documentation aligns with regulatory requirements. Process automation in healthcare executes processes consistently and logs every action, improving data accuracy and providing an audit trail crucial for compliance with standards such as HIPAA. RPA also enhances data accuracy and helps with HIPAA/GDPR compliance through the provision of clear audit logs. RPA also strengthens regulatory compliance by ensuring accurate documentation and audit readiness.

Some of these benefits are displayed in Figure 2.7 [15].

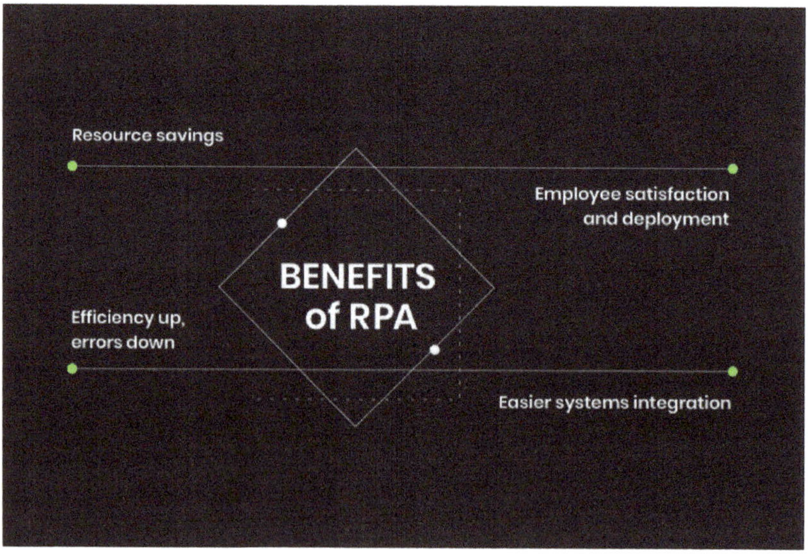

Figure 2.7 Some of these benefits of RPA [15].

2.6 Challenges

Implementing RPA in healthcare comes with its fair share of challenges. The most frequent challenges are the inconsistency and complexity of the processes, the substandard quality of the data, the resistance of the personnel, the insecurity of the data, and the long-term maintenance of the automations. Many healthcare processes still involve manual paperwork, which can make it difficult for RPA bots to extract and process relevant information efficiently. One major limitation of RPA is that it requires human initiation in certain steps due to security constraints. Other challenges include the following [12,14,16]:

- *Implementation Cost:* Cost reduction is another area where RPA faces obstacles in the healthcare sector. While automation can help reduce administrative costs, there are initial implementation costs associated with setting up an RPA system, training staff, and integrating it into existing workflows. The total cost of implementing RPA can range from $5,000 to $300,000, depending on various factors such as the complexity of tasks being automated and the size of the organization. Organizations should carefully consider their budgetary constraints before adopting RPA solutions. Even after implementation, bots require maintenance and oversight, which entail cost.

- *Resistance to Change:* Some staff members may worry about job displacement or the learning curve of using automation tools. Organizations must create clear communication and training strategies to foster adoption.

- *Complexity:* One challenge is the complexity of data management and the existing IT ecosystems. Healthcare organizations deal with vast amounts of patient information, and ensuring that this data is accurately processed and protected can be a daunting task for RPA systems. The verification of insurance coverage and claims processing often involves complex rules and regulations that require human intervention for accurate decision-making. Many hospitals rely on legacy systems that lack standardized interfaces, making it difficult for RPA bots to interact with EHRs, billing software, and compliance tools. Healthcare systems often require extensive customization for automation to function effectively.
- *Data Security:* Data security is a significant concern. Handling patient data raises serious privacy concerns. Healthcare institutions handle sensitive patient information governed by stringent regulations. While RPA enhances compliance by automating audit logs and access controls, it also introduces vulnerabilities if not implemented securely. Unauthorized data access, system misconfigurations, and weak encryption can expose protected health information.
- *Workforce Adaptation:* Workforce adaptation is another challenge, as automation reshapes job roles. While RPA is designed to augment human efforts rather than replace personnel, employees may perceive it as a threat to job security. Resistance to change can slow adoption, particularly among administrative staff unfamiliar with digital transformation initiatives. Successful implementation requires structured change management, workforce training, and clear communication about automation's role.

2.7 Future Of Robotic Process Automation In Healthcare

Robotic process automation (RPA) is not just a future concept; it has become a proven solution driving real efficiency gains in billing, scheduling, data management, and more. It is now an integral part of digital transformation in the healthcare industry. The integration of RPA into healthcare operations is transforming how institutions manage administrative and clinical workflows. It helps reduce operational costs while allowing medical professionals to focus on patient-centric tasks. With continued advancements in RPA technology, the healthcare industry has a tremendous opportunity to transform operations and deliver better outcomes for patients. As healthcare organizations continue to embrace automation, RPA is evolving beyond rule-based task execution into more advanced, intelligent systems. Researchers opine that RPA will usher in a new wave of productivity and efficiency gains in the global workforce once the technology becomes more mature and stable in the coming decade or so.

Robotic process automation in healthcare is evolving rapidly, often paired with artificial intelligence (AI) to create intelligent automation capabilities that expand applicability and value in healthcare. RPA in the healthcare sector is evolving in tandem with AI, enabling the performance of cognitive tasks, extracting insights from unstructured data, and supporting predictive analytics. These trends signal how automation will deepen its role in care delivery and operations. As healthcare systems become more complex, RPA delivers intelligent, fast solutions. As current usage of RPA in healthcare matures, we are seeing it evolve into something more than just automation—it is acquiring strategic meaning across digital health ecosystems. RPA is proving to be the technology of the future, and its goal is to provide a sustainable solution that reduces costs and delivery time, improves quality, speed, and operational efficiency of a business process [17].

2.8 Conclusion

Many healthcare providers are turning to automation solutions to streamline operations. As healthcare data continues to grow in volume and complexity, automation becomes essential. In the healthcare industry, robotic process automation employs software "bots" to take over the tedious, rule-based actions that the staff frequently perform, such as scheduling, claims processing, data entry, and updating records. RPA is being deployed across various healthcare functions to optimize efficiency, reduce administrative burdens, and enhance service delivery. It enables healthcare staff to concentrate on patient care through its capabilities, which decrease administrative work, accelerate insurance claims processing, and protect data. The success of RPA depends on measurable outcome tracking and stakeholder involvement from clinical and administrative domains, and planned maintenance and expansion strategies.

The healthcare industry has realized that automation is not a luxury; it is a survival strategy. It has finally figured out that it is cheaper, faster, and smarter to automate routine tasks and let humans do what they are best at—caring for patients. Today, RPA bots handle tasks with strict rules— claims processing, scheduling appointments, billing, and compliance reporting—with stunning accuracy. Future-looking healthcare professionals need to embrace this powerful tool and unlock its potential in improving healthcare services.

References

[1] "How robotic process automation (RPA) is optimizing 'business-as-usual'" August 2021, https://medium.com/elucidate-ai/how-robotic-process-automation-rpa-is-optimizing-business-as-usual-1c5e5c46ef43

[2] https://images.search.yahoo.com/search/images?p=images+of+healhcare+professionals&fr=mcafee&type=E210US1357G0&imgurl=https%3A%2F%2Fthumbs.dreamstime.com%2Fb%2Ftheyre-dedicated-team-healthcare-professionals-portrait-group-smiling-medical-professionals-standing-hospital-261178515.jpg#id=1&iurl=https%3A%2F%2Fthumbs.dreamstime.com%2Fb%2Ftheyre-dedicated-team-healthcare-professionals-portrait-group-smiling-medical-professionals-standing-hospital-261178515.jpg&action=click

[3] M. N. O. Sadiku and J. O. Sadiku, "Robotic process automation in healthcare," *International Journal of Trend in Research and Development,* vol. 13, no. 2, March-April, 2026, pp. 118-123

[4] N. Komitsky, "Putting robotic process automation to work in the federal government,"

https://www.managementconcepts.com/resource/putting-robotic-process-automation-to-work-in-the-federal-government/

[5] "What is robotic process automation (RPA)? How does it work?" February 2023,

https://solidpro-es.com/what-is-robotic-process-automation-rpa-how-it-works/

[6] F. Caltin, "RPA in finance," February 2020,

https://www.plutushealthinc.com/post/rpa-in-finance

[7] "Absolutely everything you need to know about robotic process automation,"

https://www.blueprism.com/guides/robotic-process-automation-rpa/

[8] S. Donnelly, "5 Benefits of robotic process automation in finance," September 2022,

https://www.financealliance.io/5-benefits-of-robotic-process-automation-in-finance/

[9] "Robotic process automation in finance," September 2023,

https://kmbs.konicaminolta.us/blog/robotic-process-automation-in-finance/

[10] "Robotic process automation in finance,"

https://planergy.com/blog/robotic-process-automation-finance/

[11] "Amazing ways that RPA can be used in healthcare," September 2021, https://www.ibm.com/think/topics/rpa-for-healthcare

[12] “The power of robotic process automation (RPA) in healthcare: Exploring use cases, benefits, and challenges,” October 2023, https://streamlinehealth.net/robotic-process-automation-healthcare/

[13] “Agentic automation & RPA in healthcare: Use cases, benefits & challenges,”

January 2026,

https://www.itransition.com/rpa/healthcare

[14] Keragon Team, “Robotic process automation in healthcare (RPA): Use cases & benefits,” July 2025, https://www.keragon.com/blog/healthcare-robotic-process-automation

[15] “What is RPA? And how does combining it with process intelligence help drive process excellence?”

https://www.celonis.com/insights/topics/what-is-rpa?utm_source=Bing&utm_medium=cpc&utm_campaign=enterprise_ai&utm_term=automation%20in%20healthcare&utm_content=605681953_en_land_whatisrpa_&_bt=&_bk=automation%20in%20healthcare&_bm=p&_bn=o&_bg=1333710141231139&msclkid=b07f9ef95d6517d3186bf7784cf79091#1-what-is-rpa

[16] “Robotic process automation case study in healthcare,” April 2025,

https://biologyinsights.com/robotic-process-automation-case-study-in-healthcare/

[17] R. Jain and R. Bhatnagar, "Robotic process automation in healthcare - A review," *International Robotics & Automation Journal,* vol. 5, no. 1, January 2019, pp. 12-14.

CHAPTER 3
ROBOTIC PROCESS AUTOMATION IN BUSINESS

"What you think, you become. What you feel, you attract. What you imagine, you create."
Buddha

3.1 Introduction

Technology continues to change society at a rapid pace, and the business sector is by no means immune. It can be a wonderful way to add value to your company. A technology that can help you to run a business is the one known as robotic process automation (RPA). RPA uses "robots" to standardize and automate repeatable business tasks. RPA bots are designed to mimic the actions of human workers, interacting with applications, databases, and systems just like a human worker would.

Robotic automation is continuing to spread into all types of businesses across the globe. Robotic process automation (RPA) involves the use of software robots or "bots" to automate repetitive, rule-based tasks that were once performed manually by employees. The application of RPA is not limited to certain areas or disciplines. Repetitive tasks exist across all functional areas in a business, and therefore, all of them are potential candidates for automation. 3.1 defines robotic process automation [1].

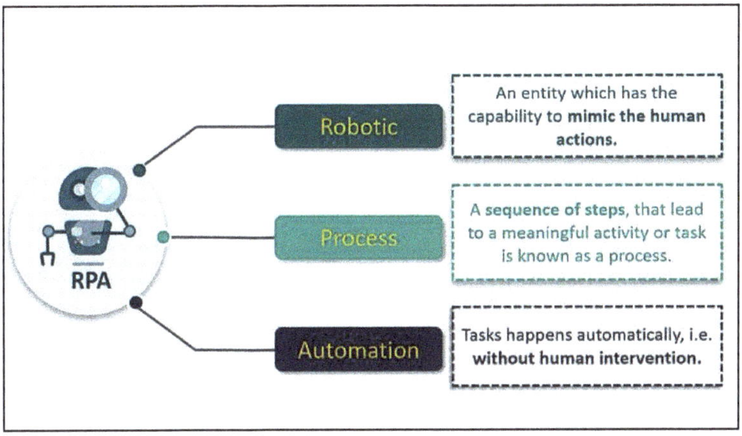

Figure 3.1 A definition of robotic process automation [1].

Every component of a business can be seen as a challenging process that can be controlled with the aid of specialized tools. In today's fast-paced business environment, companies are continuously seeking innovative ways to streamline their operations, reduce costs, and enhance overall efficiency. To reduce costs and human error, a number of processes have been automated. Automation increases productivity levels because automated techniques can do jobs faster and more efficiently than manual ones. RPA makes automation possible by mimicking human-created tasks via the graphical user interface (GUI) while keeping track of the user's actions.

Automation has changed the aspects of the business today. Robotic process automation (RPA) is the use of software robots, or bots, to help in automating certain business processes. They do so in business by maximizing cost savings and increasing efficiency. The RPA services provide data security, enhanced business efficiency, and effectiveness across various business applications without modifying the available system and infrastructure. RPA can emulate human actions and operate on any application with a user interface. The real beauty of RPA is that (unlike humans), a robot can carry out tasks continuously 24/7 and can often carry them out with higher accuracy than a human [2].

This chapter provides an overview of the benefits of RPA for businesses. It begins with introducing the concept of robotic process automation (RPA). It describes RPA in business and provides some of its applications. It highlights the benefits and challenges of RPA in business. It predicts the future of RPA in business. The last section concludes with comments.

3.2 What Is Robotic Process Automation?

Among the various forms of artificial intelligence, RPA stands out for its potential to significantly increase workforce productivity by reducing or eliminating the need to do repetitive tasks manually. Popular applications of RPA include data entry, data reconciliation, spreadsheet manipulation, systems integration, automated data reporting, analytics, email notifications, acquisitions, administrative services, finance, human resources, mission assurance, strategic communications, travel reimbursements, claims processing, and customer outreach and communications. These are just a few examples of the ways RPA is being used to remove the burden of manual, repetitive, and duplicative tasks from public service workers [3].

Robotic process automation is a form of automation software. It is a technology that can automate repetitive, rules-based tasks. Like an Excel macro operating within a spreadsheet, RPA can record actions performed across a personal computer, access systems, and perform specific tasks for human users. It uses software robots, more commonly called "bots," that mimic basic human-computer interactions. Figure 3.2 shows the symbol of RPA [4], while Figure 3.3 shows processes that RPA can automate [5]. Most industries use RPA. The government does too. Due to the repetitive nature of some tasks, the probability of human error increases. One way to eliminate errors is by using RPA.

Figure 3.2 Symbol of RPA [4].

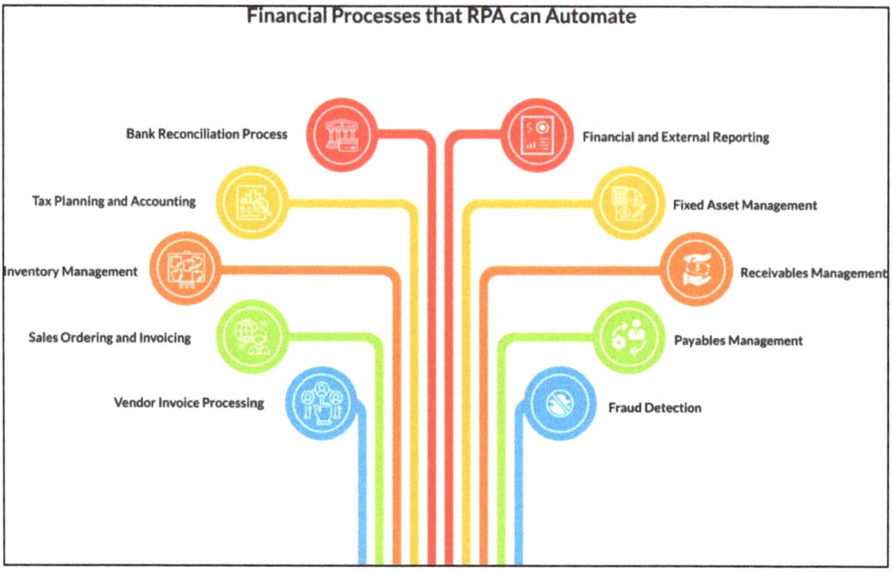

Figure 3.3 Processes that RPA can automate [5].

Robotic process automation solutions fall into three key categories: attended RPA, unattended RPA, and hybrid RPA, as shown in Figure 3.4 [6].

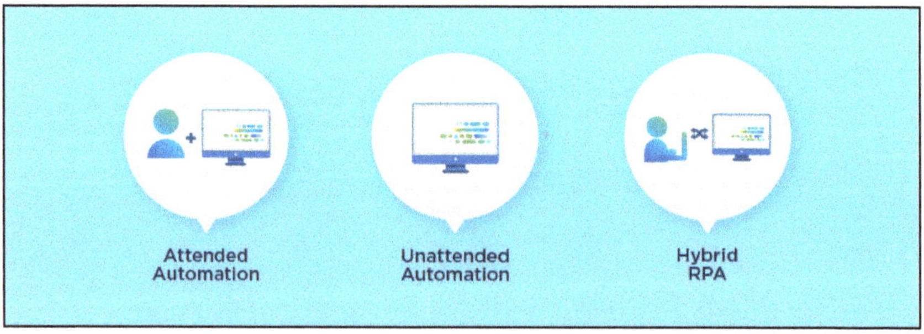

Figure 3.4 Three key categories of RPA [5].

Robotic process automation is a type of software that mimics the activity of a human being in carrying out a task within a process. It is a technology that automates repetitive tasks using software robots. RPA uses a set of automation tools to automate repetitive tasks and manual processes performed electronically. Since RPA can automate tasks that are rule-based, manual, repetitive, and tedious, delivering the highest levels of accuracy and eradicating human errors, it is a seamless fit for the finance industry. Here are some specific examples of what RPA in finance can do [7]:

- Opening emails and joining attachments
- Automatically logging into various applications on the web
- Shifting folders and files
- Copying and pasting
- Completing forms
- Collecting data from databases and the web
- Making calculations
- Connecting to system API
- Extracting structured data from documents
- Gathering stats from social media
- Following if/then decisions and rules

Some of these tasks are displayed in Figure 3.5 [6].

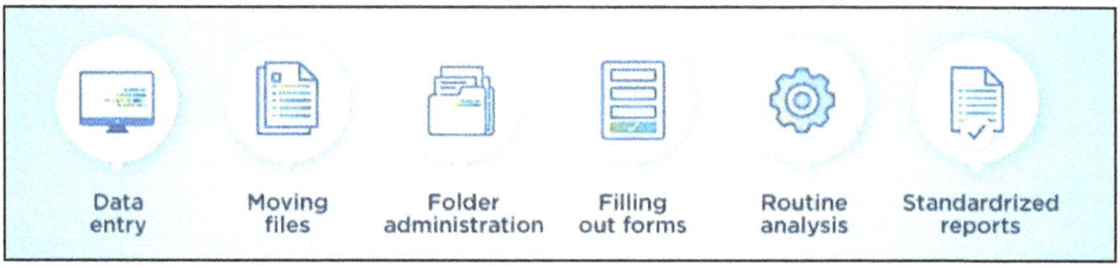

Figure 3.5 Some tasks RPA can perform [6].

At its core, robotic process automation (RPA) is a tool designed to mimic rule-based business processes, performing them seamlessly and without fatigue. RPA is a rule-driven method that is limited in its application. The technology functions much like a Microsoft Excel macro; the key difference is in power and reach. It follows set rules, similar to how an Excel macro works, to do things like move files or log into accounts. Growing as a popular solution in finance and accounting, RPA refers to software technology or "software robots" with artificial intelligence (AI) and machine learning (ML) capabilities. The "software robots" have the ability to learn and complete a high volume of rules-based, repetitive tasks and business processes. They have the capacity to operate much faster than humans, with 100% precision and reliability, working around the clock.

Finance and human resources are just two examples of departments likely to have many use cases that RPA can help solve. Some examples of good use cases for RPA in finance include processing customer orders, ensuring timely vendor payments, and managing period-end financial close processes. For human resources, some examples include employee onboarding, time tracking, and leave of absence management. Processes where human judgment is needed are not appropriate for RPA since RPA automations rely on clear, consistently applied rules [8].

Along with RPA, one should be aware of both business process automation (BPA) and digital process automation (DPA) – two commonly used automation technologies that robotics process automation can be paired with to optimize and streamline a digital transformation. BPA refers to the use of technology to automate complex, multi-step workflows, typically very specific to a company's core business functions. DPA offers dual power by automating processes from end to end and optimizing common workflows that involve external human interactions (i.e., sales, management). Separately, RPA and AI are quite powerful, but leveraging them together is undoubtedly advantageous to any financial institution. When deployed together, AI is the "brains" behind RPA's bots [9].

3.3 Robotic Process Automation In Business

The world is moving towards digital transformation, and automation is one of the most well-known solutions in digital transformation. Every business wants to automate its tasks to reduce human labor, increase the efficiency of work, focus on more complex tasks, enhance cost efficiency, etc. To shape the present and future of automation for business operations, there is a technology that is referred to as robotic process automation (RPA).

Robotic process automation (RPA) is a type of technology that we see in business. It refers to software technology that makes it easier to build and deploy software robots that mimic human interactions to make running your business easier and more efficient. It uses software "bots" to mimic human actions—such as typing, clicking, and data entry—to automate high-volume, rule-based business processes. The bots interact with customers and software, and are able to do several different tasks, taking these data-heavy or repetitive tasks away from human staff members. For example, simple, repetitive tasks such as copying and pasting information between business systems can be massively accelerated when completed using robots.

In today's evolving technological landscape, businesses are increasingly turning to automation to enhance efficiency and reduce operational costs. Organizations across all industries are leveraging RPA to streamline operations and reduce costs. Robotic process automation in business operations refers to the use of software robots to automate repetitive, rule-based tasks within an organization's systems. Once RPA is in place, employees can focus on more strategic tasks, such as developing long-term business strategies, setting goals, and aligning resources to meet organizational objectives—all of which are imperative to a business's success. One of RPA's defining characteristics is its versatility, making it a transformative force across a spectrum of industries. From government services to manufacturing, RPA finds applications in streamlining processes, reducing errors, and amplifying productivity. RPA is being used across multiple sectors, including banking, healthcare, telecom, and business functions, to revolutionize the way we work.

3.4 Applications Of Robotic Process Automation In Business

Robotic process automation can be used in business for a variety of different purposes. It

It is often used in back-office operations, such as finance, accounting, and HR departments, to improve efficiency, reduce errors, and free up human workers to focus on more strategic and value-adding tasks. It is also used in customer service operations, such as chatbots, to provide automated support to customers. Figure 3.6 shows some use cases of RPA [10]. The universal applicability of RPA underscores its versatility and adaptability, allowing it to address specific challenges unique to each industry. Common areas of applications of RPA in business include the following [10-16]:

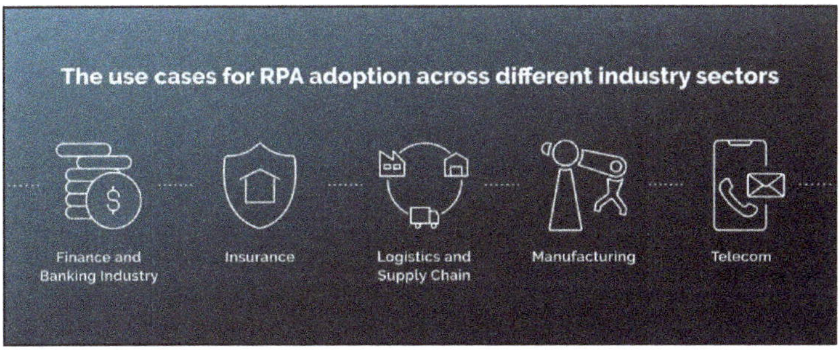

Figure 3.6 Some use cases of RPA [10].

- *Finance*: In finance industries, RPA may be used for purposes like automating governance, processing invoices, or reconciling accounts. It is typically used for automation and can automate a variety of tasks to save time for the human members of the team. In finance and banking, RPA can allow bots to extract data from invoices, validate them against purchase orders, and initiate payment. Financial services will further integrate RPA with AI to enhance customer service and compliance monitoring. In the dynamic landscape of the banking sector, RPA emerges as a transformative force, revolutionizing various aspects of financial operations.
- *Accounting*: The accounting industry is still trying to figure out how automation fits in with its digital transformation journeys. RPA has already garnered interest from public accounting firms, particularly with respect to taxation, advisory, and assurance services. For example, a significant portion of tax activities, such as the calculation of book-tax differences and the preparation of tax returns, has been successfully automated by RPA software robots. RPA is a common tool to generate and send sales invoices to customers autonomously, quickly, and accurately. It can also create accurate production reports to support data-driven decision-making.
- *Auditing*: RPA is a form of process improvement using technology. When applied to auditing, RPA is expected to not only replace manual and mundane audit tasks but also to motivate the re-engineering of audit processes. RPA can be programmed to calculate whether the price and quantity are different across sales invoices, sales orders, and shipping documents, and to generate alerts for sales transactions that contain differences in price and quantity. By automating these

procedures, auditors can reallocate their time to more value-added activities, which will inherently increase audit quality. By leveraging RPA software, auditors can obtain a better understanding of the client's business operations.

- *Healthcare*: Matching appointment requests with the actual availability of doctors is a long and tedious process, which must take into account the patient's health conditions and the specialists' schedules. This planning can be streamlined with healthcare solutions powered by RPA. By automating the collection and processing of patients' data, RPA-based tools can keep these records constantly updated and quickly extract them from databases.
- *Manufacturing*: Manufacturing leaders began to incorporate more RPA to streamline entire processes and improve compliance. By adopting RPA, manufacturers can reduce human errors and increase productivity. Companies in the manufacturing industry were the early adopters of automation, implementing robots and processing lines to perform daily production activities in the plant. One well-known German automaker recently implemented RPA and successfully automated a total of 28 different tasks, including payment and refunds processing, reconciling of forecast vs actual expenditures, customs import processing, the generation of commercial finance contracts, and many more. Manufacturing automation in Industry 4.0 is shifting toward mass production and mass customization via human–robot collaboration.
- *Insurance*: RPA is already assisting many insurance providers in accelerating processes ranging from customer onboarding to underwriting. It helps in increasing productivity and also creating a better customer experience.

- *Telecommunication*: The telecoms industry is among the most advanced in implementing RPA. The industry leverages RPA to enhance operational efficiency, improve customer service, and ensure the seamless management of complex networks. RPA, combined with AI processing, can help automate network optimization so that faults are addressed in real-time with minimal human intervention. RPA can also help telecom companies more smartly manage content offerings. Telecom companies are shifting from manual to automated processing of customer data to perform multiple tasks.
- *Customer service*: RPA bots can be used to provide automated support to customers through chatbots or voice assistants, answering common queries and directing customers to the appropriate resources.
- *Supply Chain Management*: RPA extends its transformative impact to supply chain management, optimizing various facets of the intricate network that connects manufacturers, suppliers, and consumers. RPA bots can be used to automate supply chain processes such as order processing, inventory management, and shipment tracking.
- *Retail*: In the retail sector, RPA drives efficiency in various operational aspects, offering a competitive edge in a rapidly evolving market. The retail sector can significantly benefit from RPA implementation. The advanced automation solution is successfully used for product analytics and customer satisfaction. RPA helps collect sales data and automate certain aspects of retail business intelligence.

3.5 Benefits

Primarily used in finance, HR, and customer service, RPA boosts efficiency, reduces errors, and cuts operational costs by handling tasks like invoice processing, data migration, and employee onboarding 24/7. The integration of RPA into business operations offers numerous benefits. By automating mundane and repetitive tasks, RPA frees up employees to focus on more strategic and creative work. Some of RPA's benefits are faster processing, cost savings, reduced errors, improved productivity, better compliance and consistency, and enhanced customer satisfaction. All the usual repetitive, frequent, mundane, and high-volume tasks can benefit from RPA. Other benefits include the following [11]:

- *Reduce Costs*: One of the big benefits of robotic process automation is that it can decrease the money spent by a business. RPA can significantly reduce operational costs. Software robots are faster than humans at performing repetitive tasks, leading to reduced labor costs and faster throughput. When a business asks a human team member to complete a task, this costs the company money and can also be affected by errors. RPA is a more cost-effective option when it comes to certain tasks, like data-heavy tasks, rather than hiring a full-time employee who would work on these tasks.
- *Save Time:* RPA implementations can help your business by saving time. We have all heard the saying that "time is money!" RPA can complete some of the more time-intensive tasks that human employees would otherwise have to do themselves. By saving time, you are also increasing efficiency in all of the facets of your business that the RPA touches. RPA helps to

increase the productivity of a human worker and the business as a whole.

- *Reduce Errors:* Human error is a common cause of inefficiencies in business processes. RPA software tools can help to reduce errors that may have occurred when human workers were handling these different and likely complicated tasks. It is true that there are areas where mistakes just cannot happen— if they do, they can have very serious effects.
- *Enhance Customer Satisfaction:* Customer satisfaction is key to any of the businesses, regardless of the industry that you are in. If your customers are unhappy, this is another factor that can affect your bottom line. This is why it is so great that RPA technology is able to help you increase and enhance your customer experience and customer satisfaction.
- *Streamline Business Operations*: RPA software tools can help to streamline your business operations, and by streamlining your business operations, you can transform your business! RPA is considered to be one of the best and easiest ways to make changes in your business to begin transforming different areas for the better. It can also help to first give you proof of concept before you continue to introduce new changes or initiatives. RPA brings efficiency to bureaucratic workflows by automating routine administrative tasks such as data entry, document processing, and form filling
- *Transparency*: Robotic process automation software is suitable for creating regular reports in which the data must be extracted from several systems and displayed in a structured manner. Through automated analyses of large amounts of data, RPA can also be used as an early warning system if, for example, certain data is read out regularly and reported.

- *Flexibility:* RPA is applicable across all industries and organizations, from large corporations to small start-ups. It is easily scalable and can handle any task with a rule-based element and defined by repeatable actions.

Some benefits of RPA are depicted in Figure 3.7 [17].

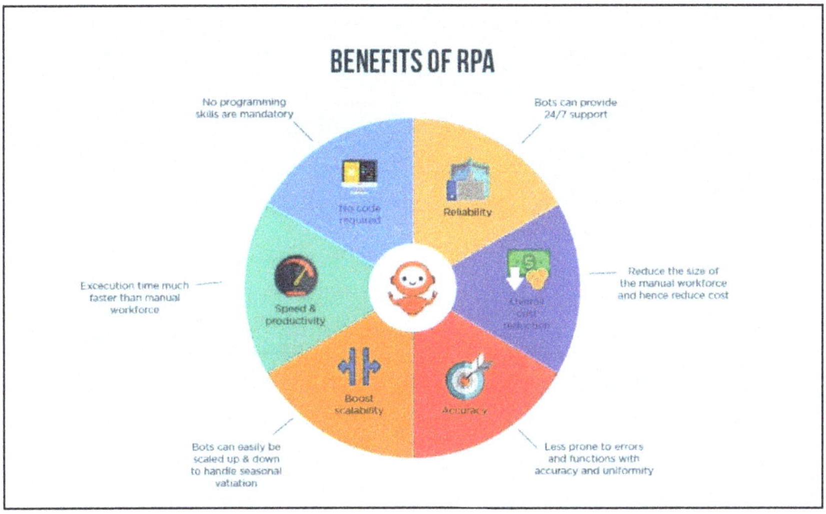

Figure 3.7 Some benefits of RPA [17].

3.6 Challenges

As organizations increasingly adopt RPA, they also need individuals with expertise in RPA tools and implementations. RPA systems are static and require manual updates when processes change. They cannot adapt to new inputs or learn from data. For the automation of complex business processes, RPA is not suitable with the present state of the art. Other challenges include the following [18,19]:

- *High Cost:* Pricing is always an important factor while implementing any technology solutions. Automation is a new technology that has developed in recent years, so it takes too much cost. The pricing of RPA-powered solutions depends on various factors like the complexity of the processes being automated and the chosen vendor; factors like customization needs and ongoing maintenance can significantly impact the total cost.
- *Complexity:* Implementing RPA can be challenging, given both the potential complexity of legacy business processes and the level of change management that can be required for RPA to succeed. Implementing RPA can be straightforward for simple tasks, but it becomes complex and less effective as processes require more decision-making and variability. Many implementations fail because design and change are poorly managed. Processes that require complex business decisions and a large number of outcomes demand highly complex automation.
- *Compliance:* Compliance with regulations and data security is paramount in government operations. RPA helps ensure adherence to regulatory frameworks by automating compliance checks and audits. There are a lot of governance challenges related to instantiating a single bot, let alone thousands. RPA can introduce security and compliance risks, particularly when handling sensitive data.
- *RPA is Static*: RPA is designed for automating specific, repetitive tasks within existing workflows, operating strictly under set rules. It follows a predefined set of instructions. If a process changes even slightly, the RPA bot must be reprogrammed. RPA would require separate rule-based bots for different inventory tasks and frequent updates when

product demand changes. For example, an RPA bot for invoice processing will fail if a vendor slightly changes the format of their invoice. RPA is purely a task automation tool, executing routine processes without making any decisions.

- *Scalability*: While RPA promises adaptability, some tools may struggle to scale, especially when interfacing with outdated legacy systems. This can lead to operational challenges as businesses grow. RPA is not too scalable for now, as it takes code development for most of the use cases. However, no-code RPA is one of the most useful future trends shaping the future of RPA for business operations. This allows normal people to use drag-and-drop interfaces to develop RPA solutions for their business in the future. This overall enhances the scalability of RPA.
- *Data Quality*: RPA systems rely heavily on data. Poor data quality can lead to errors and inefficiencies in automated processes.

3.7 Future Of Robotic Process Automation In Business

Today's automation trend is about applying all relevant technologies to automate business processes as much as possible. Robotic process automation services involve the use of software robots to automate repetitive, rule-based tasks within business processes. RPA is gaining in popularity and is more and more willingly used by companies from various industries. It is revolutionizing business and industry productivity. The landscape of RPA is evolving rapidly as tech in the field continues to advance. Its processes are all about growth, and we will definitely see lots of growth in what it can help us achieve in the next few years. Organizations today are beginning to realize the evolution of automation and are coming forward to implement RPA in their businesses. This has led to a revolution in the RPA global market value.

Since RPA is not limited to simple, rule-based tasks, it is starting to become integrated with artificial intelligence, machine learning, and natural language processing. This combination will gain traction and popularity as businesses experience what it can do for them. RPA tries to reduce business management costs through faster activities and more efficient processes that may support many businesses in the future.

3.8 Conclusion

Robotic process automation (RPA) is a technology that uses software bots to replicate and automate repetitive, rule-based tasks that follow logical steps. It refers to the use of software robots to automate repetitive and rule-based tasks in business processes. It provides organizations with the ability to reduce staffing costs and human error. More business leaders are turning to robotic process automation to eliminate tedious tasks, streamline enterprise operations, reduce costs, and free corporate workers to focus on higher-value work. RPA is transforming how businesses operate.

RPA has evolved over recent years. To attain a competitive edge and continue relevant to the industry front-runners, most large enterprises have implemented RPA, and it has positively proved its utility in several scenarios. RPA's scope is limited, and various requirements must be met for it to be applied efficiently. It can automate tasks through complex workflows without requiring extensive upfront planning or design. More information about robotic process automation in business can be found in the books [20-24].

References

[1] "How robotic process automation (RPA) is optimizing 'business-as-usual'" August 2021,

https://medium.com/elucidate-ai/how-robotic-process-automation-rpa-is-optimizing-business-as-usual-1c5e5c46ef43

[2] N. Komitsky, "Putting robotic process automation to work in the federal government,"

https://www.managementconcepts.com/resource/putting-robotic-process-automation-to-work-in-the-federal-government/

[3] M. N. O. Sadiku and J. O. Sadiku, "Robotic process automation in business," *International Journal of Trend in Research and Development*, vol. 13, no. 1, January-February 2026, pp. 110-115.

[4] "What is robotic process automation (RPA)? How does it work?" February 2023,

https://solidpro-es.com/what-is-robotic-process-automation-rpa-how-it-works/

[5] F. Caltin, "RPA in finance," February 2020,

https://www.plutushealthinc.com/post/rpa-in-finance

[6] "Absolutely everything you need to know about robotic process automation,"

https://www.blueprism.com/guides/robotic-process-automation-rpa/

[7] S. Donnelly, "5 Benefits of robotic process automation in finance," September 2022,

https://www.financealliance.io/5-benefits-of-robotic-process-automation-in-finance/

[8] "Robotic process automation in finance," September 2023,

https://kmbs.konicaminolta.us/blog/robotic-process-automation-in-finance/

[9] "Robotic process automation in finance,"

https://planergy.com/blog/robotic-process-automation-finance/

[10] K. Khan, "Building intelligent enterprises: Getting started with robotic process automation," February 2025,

https://www.trantorinc.com/blog/robotic-process-automation

[11] "What is robotic process automation (RPA) – 7 ways it can transform your business,"

https://evolvedmetrics.com/what-is-robotic-process-automation-rpa/

[12] "Robotic process automation (RPA) for manufacturing: Driving efficiency further," April 2020,

https://www.themanufacturer.com/articles/robotic-process-automation-rpa-for-manufacturing/

[13] W. A. Rousan, "Unleashing the power of RPA: Exploring diverse use cases for business transformation," December 2023,

https://datahubanalytics.com/rpa-exploring-diverse-use-cases-for-business-transformation/

[14] "Bots are not coming, they're here! The impact of robotic process automation (RPA) on the accounting profession," November 2023,

https://poole.ncsu.edu/thought-leadership/article/bots-are-not-coming-theyre-here-the-impact-of-robotic-process-automation-rpa-on-the-accounting-profession/

[15] "Robotic process automation use cases for 5 industries and how to apply them," April 2023,

https://www.openaccessgovernment.org/robotic-process-automation-use-cases-industries/158205/

[16] M. A. Vasarhelyi and A. M. Rozario, "How robotic process automation is transforming accounting and auditing," July 2018,

https://www.cpajournal.com/2018/07/02/how-robotic-process-automation-is-transforming-accounting-and-auditing/

[17] A. Sureka, "Introduction to RPA - The future of business process management,"

https://www.clariontech.com/platform-blog/introduction-to-robotic-process-automation-rpa-the-future-of-business-process-management

[18] "What is RPA? A revolution in business process automation,"

https://www.cio.com/article/227908/what-is-rpa-robotic-process-automation-explained.html

[19] "The future of robotic process automation in business operations," February 2025,

https://www.roboticstomorrow.com/news/2025/02/26/the-future-of-robotic-process-automation-in-business-operations/24301/

[20] C. Czarnecki and P. Fettke (eds.), *Robotic Process Automation: Management, Technology, Applications.* De Gruyter, 2021.

[21] C. Juarez, *Unleashing Efficiency: The Power of Robotic Process Automation (RPA).* Independently Published, 2023.

[22] H. Mahey, *Robotic Process Automation with Automation Anywhere: Techniques to Fuel Business Productivity And Intelligent Automation Using RPA.* Packt Publishing, 2020.

[23] T. Taulli, *The Robotic Process Automation Handbook: A Guide to Implementing RPA Systems.* Apress, 2020.

[24] R. Fantina, A. Storozhuk, and K. Goyal, *Introducing Robotic Process Automation to Your Organization: A Guide for Business Leaders*. Apress, 2021.

CHAPTER 4
ROBOTIC PROCESS AUTOMATION IN FINANCE

"Never depend on a single income. Invest to create a second source."
Warren Buffett

4.1 Introduction

Financial organizations are inundated with paper accumulation. Performing such tasks manually is not only time-consuming but also leads to errors. This is where robotic process automation (RPA) comes into play. RPA is a simple and easy-to-use software that uses software robots to mimic human actions and complete tasks. By substituting humans with RPA bots for undertaking manual and monotonous tasks, business executives are successfully curtailing manual intervention, thus transforming elements from expenditures and staffing issues to efficiency and performance levels. Figure 4.1 shows some business executives [1].

Figure 4.1 Some business executives [1].

The digital era is changing the way businesses operate, and RPA stands at the forefront of this evolution. RPA automates repetitive business processes across a wide range of industries, including banking, accounting, IT, human resources, government, transportation, insurance, communications, and healthcare, as shown in Figure 4.2 [2]. The reason to use RPA in these industries is to improve data entry and calculations. For years, finance teams have used robotic process automation (RPA) to improve the speed, efficiency, and accuracy of specific tasks. RPA in finance extends automation into banking and accounting operations to reduce the amount of human labor required to process transactions. It liberates the workforce from tedious, monotonous tasks and transitions it towards processes requiring more thinking.

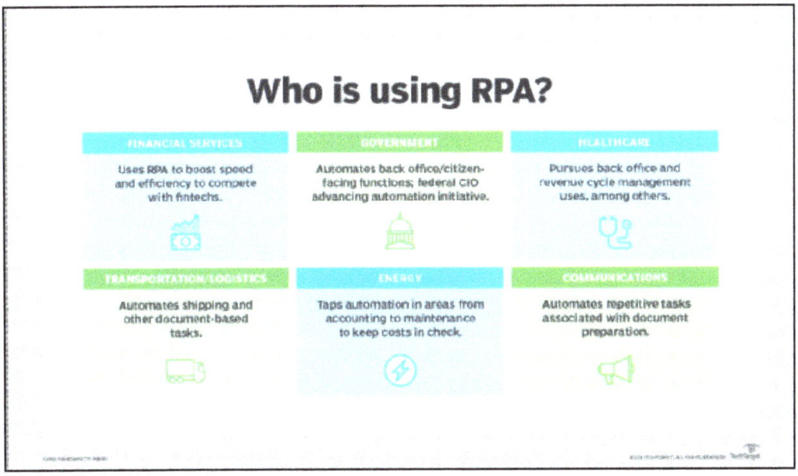

Figure 4.2 RPA automates repetitive business processes across a wide range of industries [2].

Robotic process automation (RPA) is computer-coded software that automates repetitive tasks and processes. It is important for companies seeking to transform themselves by doing "more" with "less." Used in a variety of industries, RPA refers to the use of low-code software "bots" to handle the repetitive, time-consuming tasks of human workers — such as invoice processing, data entry, compliance reporting, etc. The main focus of RPA in finance is to replace repetitive and rule-based tasks. Software robots can do many amazing things to make the life of a finance professional much easier [3].

This chapter highlights the use of robotic process automation (RPA) in the finance industry. It begins with explaining what RPA is all about. It covers some applications of RPA in finance. It mentions the benefits and challenges of RPA in finance. The last section concludes with comments.

4.2 What Is Robotic Process Automation?

The finance industry is process-oriented. Financial institutions undertake various business processes such as revenue management, financial planning, accounts payable and receivable, and cash disbursement, among others, on a daily basis. Every financial activity goes through a rigorous process to avoid human errors. Figure 4.3 shows the symbol of RPA in finance [4], while Figure 4.4 shows processes that RPA can automate [5]. However, due to the repetitive nature of the tasks, the probability of human error increases. One way to eliminate errors in the finance industry is by using RPA.

Figure 4.3 Symbol of RPA in finance [4].

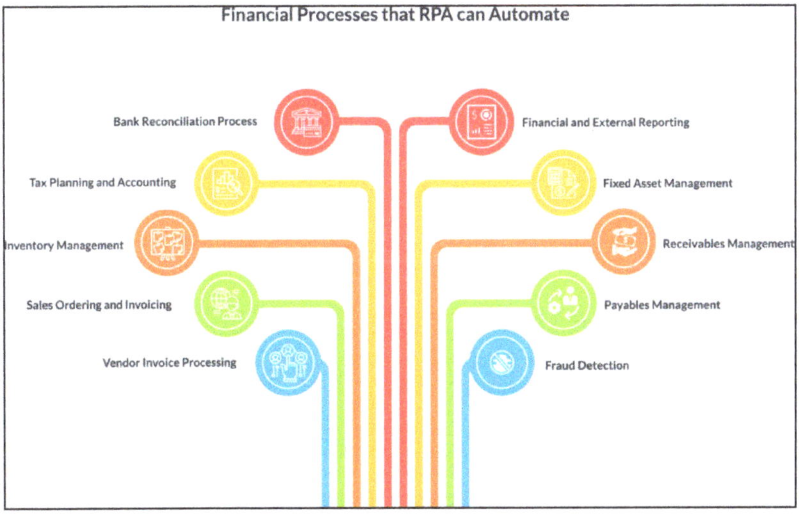

Figure 4.4 Processes that RPA can automate [5].

Robotic process automation is a type of software that mimics the activity of a human being in carrying out a task within a process. It is a technology that automates repetitive tasks using software robots. RPA uses a set of automation tools to automate repetitive tasks and manual processes performed electronically. Since RPA can automate tasks that are rule-based, manual, repetitive, and tedious, delivering the highest levels of accuracy and eradicating human errors, it is a seamless fit for the finance industry. Here are some specific examples of what RPA in finance can do [6]:

- Opening emails and joining attachments
- Automatically logging into various applications on the web
- Shifting folders and files
- Copying and pasting
- Completing forms
- Collecting data from databases and the web
- Making calculations
- Connecting to system API
- Extracting structured data from documents
- Gathering stats from social media
- Following if/then decisions and rules

Some of these tasks are displayed in Figure 4.5 [7].

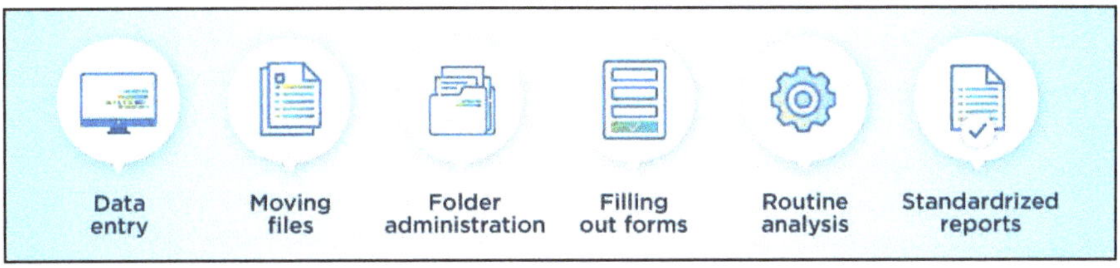

Figure 4.5 Some tasks RPA can perform [7].

At its core, robotic process automation (RPA) is a tool designed to mimic rule-based business processes, performing them seamlessly and without fatigue. RPA is a rule-driven method that is limited in its application. The technology functions much like a Microsoft Excel macro; the key difference is in power and reach. It follows set rules, similar to how an Excel macro works, to do things like move files or log into accounts. Growing as a popular solution in finance and accounting, RPA refers to software technology or "software robots" with artificial intelligence (AI) and machine learning (ML) capabilities. The "software robots" have the ability to learn and complete a high volume of rules-based, repetitive tasks and business processes. They have the capacity to operate much faster than humans, with 100% precision and reliability, working around the clock.

Finance and human resources are just two examples of departments likely to have many use cases that RPA can help solve. Some examples of good use cases for RPA in finance include processing customer orders, ensuring timely vendor payments, and managing period-end financial close processes. For human resources, some examples include employee onboarding, time tracking, and leave of absence management. Processes where human judgment is needed are not appropriate for RPA since RPA automations rely on clear, consistently applied rules [8].

Along with RPA, one should be aware of both business process automation (BPA) and digital process automation (DPA) – two commonly used automation technologies that robotics process automation can be paired with to optimize and streamline a digital transformation. BPA refers to the use of technology to automate complex, multi-step workflows, typically very specific to a company's core business functions. DPA offers dual power by automating processes from end to end and optimizing common workflows that involve external human interactions (i.e., sales, management). Separately, RPA and AI are quite powerful, but leveraging them together is undoubtedly advantageous to any financial institution. When deployed together, AI is the "brains" behind RPA's bots [9].

4.3 Applications of Robotic Process Automation in Finance

Automation can be deployed across a wide range of technology systems, functional areas of the business, and perform a wide range of tasks. RPA's usage is growing in the finance and accounting departments because it is effective in handling repetitive, mundane, back-office tasks. With RPA in finance and accounting, professionals are able to allocate more of their time to high-value, strategic, and advisory roles to help organizations remain competitive, innovative, and profitable. RPA can be applied to various finance and accounting processes, such as invoice processing, reconciliation, reporting, budgeting, forecasting, and tax compliance. Figure 4.6 shows some RPA use cases in the finance sector [10]. A few examples of financial processes that you should be able to automate include the following [11-13]:

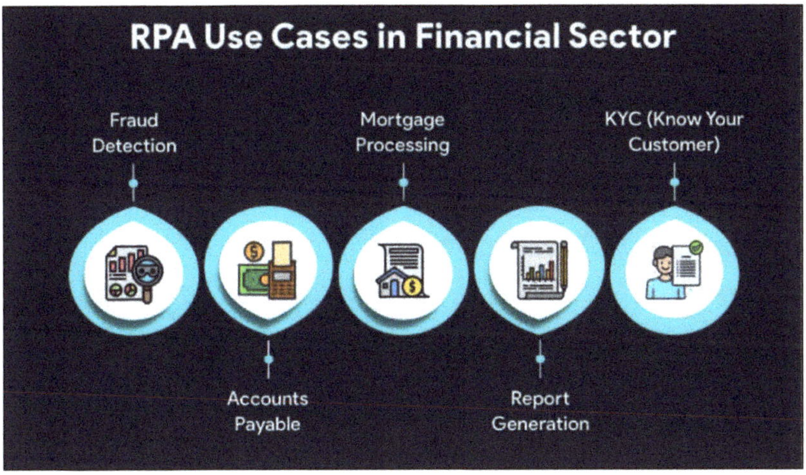

Figure 4.6 Some RPA use cases in the finance sector [10].

- *Accounts Receivable:* Properly managing accounts receivable is directly related to cash flow, so it is of utmost importance. There is a high margin for error if a single record is entered incorrectly, which will affect payment. As such, robotic process automation can be utilized to automate the creation, sending, and tracking of invoice payments. Robotic accounting is a form of RPA in the accounting field. RPA should be seen as more of a robotic arm to assist accounting departments and optimize operations. RPA in accounting can be primarily "internal"–i.e., automating tasks you would otherwise have expert employees perform–or "external"–

which involves direct interactions with customers. It automates data analysis tasks and identification of trends, anomalies, and potential opportunities. Figure 4.7 shows the symbol of RPA in accounting [13].

Figure 4.7 Symbol of RPA in accounting [13].

- *Accounts Payable:* Accounts payable (AP) involves tracking money owed to vendors or suppliers and making sure that payments are made on schedule. Accounts payable, like accounts receivable, is a key repetitive function of accounting teams. Accounting departments are often plagued with the inevitabilities of human error, cumbersome processes, and repetitive tasks. Accounts payable is a critical, repetitive function of finance teams, which is time-consuming when done manually. Not only do employees need to validate the fields, but they have to digitize vendor invoices and then process the payment. When RPA is utilized in AP automation software, incoming invoices are distributed to the appropriate recipient automatically. Late payments can be avoided by scheduling reminders.

- *Public Accounting:* Robotics and AI are used in a variety of public accounting applications that include tax automation, consultancy, assurance assistance, reconciliation, and analytical functions. They also serve to substitute traditional evaluation and auditing techniques. The most transformational use of robotics in public accounting is in assessments and auditing. RPA and AI have dramatically enhanced automation in tax, advisory, and assurance services, enabling accountants to provide more extensive and reliable advice faster.
- *Account Reconciliation:* Account reconciliation is one of the most important tasks in a finance department because it confirms that a company's general ledger balances are accurate. One of the chief challenges in this domain is juxtaposing company accounts with bank statements. This meticulous process demands acute attention to detail and often involves the tedious task of navigating between different systems. RPA can simplify and expedite this reconciliation. RPA in the financial industry can help companies balance their accounts and provide accurate financial statements.
- *Auditing:* RPA helps auditors by accurately performing some tasks, such as reconciliations. Since auditing is a type of process improvement using technology, RPA is expected to replace repetitive and manual audit tasks. It is also intended to motivate the re-engineering of audit systems. Due to the highly regulated nature of the industry, RPA for auditing remains in its early stages. RPA is a disruptive and dramatic change to current audit practices that enables auditors to operate at a higher level and perform more efficient work.

- *Data Management:* Most organizations operate with data in various systems. Data is vital in every industry, especially finance and accounting. Data is a paramount asset within businesses, but when it is separated and hard to access, it proves useless. Robotics process automation is a great solution to improve data management. RPA bots can be tasked to easily move, collect, and transfer data between systems to execute processes, conduct analysis, and generate insightful reports.
- *Know Your Customer (KYC):* KYC (know your customer) is a time-consuming procedure mandatory for banks to perform for every customer. KYC is a laborious but crucial requirement for banking and financial service providers. Each customer needs to be examined to ensure they are who they say they are and that they are not attempting to conduct fraudulent activity. Becoming more prevalent in the digital age, finance departments and institutions are enlisting KYC to verify customers' identities, and assess and monitor customer risk. Not only is KYC costly in time, but many companies are also faced with compliance sanctions. RPA can cut out this manual work and save time and money by eliminating the tendency for human error and uncertainty associated with KYC processes.
- *Fraud Detection:* Identity theft, banking fraud, money laundering, and other types of malfeasance are of major concern for finance teams across all industries. To help detect and prevent fraud, financial institutions need the right cybersecurity technology for due diligence checks. In accordance with recent statistics, the anti-money laundering process is "highly manual." Because bringing money laundering activities to a halt is time-sensitive, RPA

technology would be a great solution. RPA helps in anti-money laundering investigations by establishing an "if-then" approach to identify potential red flags. RPA improves the speed and accuracy of fraud detection. In terms of fraud detection, it has been estimated that analysts are spending 90% of their time collecting and entering fraud-related data into the system.

- *Invoicing Processing:* Timely, accurate invoice processing is a cornerstone of an AP department because it allows finance teams to track how much money the company owes to vendors and to properly approve payments. Processing invoices is a labor-intensive and error-prone task. Between handling and routing invoices (especially paper formats), managing vendor disputes, reconciling duplicate entries, and stringent compliance adherence, the hurdles are plenty. Automation can help enhance and speed it up by scanning, extracting, and analyzing data from invoices, reducing mistakes and freeing up accountants' bandwidth. RPA is equipped to tackle these challenges head-on. Its precision-centric approach can clear backlogs, ensuring the finance department is always abreast of the latest.
- *Expense Management:* Manual processes in validating and reimbursing employee expenses can quickly spiral into an administrative mess. Mismanaged reimbursements can strain payroll departments and lead to internal disputes. With RPA, these challenges are mitigated. The automation ensures swift and accurate processing, always in alignment with company guidelines. By standardizing expense management, organizations can instill better financial discipline.
- *Mortgage Processing:* Processing mortgages and loans is among the most common uses of RPA in banking and finance.

Closing a mortgage loan can take up to 60 days, with loan officers required to go through steps including employment verification, credit checks, and inspections. This is because the banks require credible information on the customer's previous finances, loans, properties, and other details. Considering the efficiency and reliability of RPA systems, banks can process and validate the required information within a short time.

- *Report Generation:* A common request for many financial services is the generation of reports. Financial reporting requires precision, particularly when providing reports and forecasts to stakeholders. RPA can efficiently gather and analyze data from diverse sources, present it in a coherent format, and generate highly accurate reports. In order to remain compliant with regulations, banks are required to prepare reports regarding their performance and activities. These reports contain vast amounts of data, making them time-consuming to produce and (potentially) filled with errors. RPA and banking can remove these issues by automatically gathering data from the necessary sources, arranging it into a coherent format, and producing the reports with no mistakes.

4.4 Benefits

There are numerous benefits of adopting RPA technology in the finance industry. RPA software performs monotonous tasks at a level of accuracy, speed, and scale that humans cannot compete with. Driving greater efficiency and compliance while reducing human error are just a few of the reasons RPA in finance is so beneficial. Incorporating automation is not just about embracing the future; it is about ensuring survival and growth. Other important benefits of RPA include the following [5]

- *Cost-Effectiveness:* Cost savings are critical to the finance industry. Automation can streamline processes and reduce the need for manual labor, leading to cost savings. According to industry research, RPA can drive 25-50% cost savings by automating rule-based, repetitive tasks. Implementing RPA in finance does not require any significant modifications in infrastructure. Many companies that have implemented robotic process automation in finance see substantial ROI.
- *Increase Efficiency:* Humans are simply prone to mistakes, especially when manually processing invoices or sorting Excel spreadsheets. RPA bots increase the efficiency of financial processes. With RPA bots, business executives can make their processes quick, productive, and highly efficient. RPA reduces processing times and streamlines various processes across the finance function.
- *Boost Productivity:* By replacing humans with RPA bots for repetitive and mundane tasks, CFOs can achieve optimum efficiency. Task automation would reduce human error and significantly improve productivity. Maximum efficiency and improved productivity lead to increased gains for the business.
- *Accessibility:* It is easy to buy into the misconception that RPA is only for the big players. Rather, RPA technologies have become enormously more accessible for smaller, regional accounting firms, even ones with relatively modest IT setups.
- *Availability:* Whether banks want to eliminate manual intervention or achieve higher accuracy at low cost, RPA bots

work 24/7 to complete the tasks assigned to them. Thus, their availability is unencumbered.

- *Risk and Compliance Reporting:* In finance, remaining compliant requires a high level of detail. RPA helps banks and financial institutions in generating reports of complete audit trails for every process, reducing business risks and ensuring compliance. Keeping up with the changing regulatory standards is crucial for CFOs in order to successfully handle financial and accounting processes. RPA allows CFOs to keep track of the regulatory standards and alleviate non-compliance risks, ensuring that financial processes abide by the regulations.
- *Faster Implementation:* With a drag-and-drop feature, RPA tools are faster to implement. Using RPA bots, organization scan easily automates their financial processes and maintain automation workflows without many coding requirements. Faster information processing ultimately enables enhanced customer service.
- *No Infrastructure Cost:* One of the major benefits of RPA is that it does not require any infrastructure cost. Due to its automation capabilities, the hardware and maintenance costs of RPA infrastructure are zero.
- *Business Growth With Legacy Data:* With RPA techniques, the finance industry is using both legacy and new data to bridge between the financial processes. This kind of effort and availability of essential data in one system enables fintechs to generate faster and better reports for business growth.
- *Receiving Budget Approval:* CFOs often deal with business proposals that are without merit in terms of potential overall benefits or recognizable ROI. However, the RPA concept

enables financial leaders to create a business case, delivering significant value to their company.

- *Accuracy Eliminates Human Error:* In the intricate world of finance, where every figure and decimal count, the importance of accuracy cannot be overstated. Humans make mistakes. Reducing the margin of error is one of the best benefits of automating key financial processes. Human error can cause upheaval and negative consequences that could ripple throughout the business. RPA can take human error off the table and help to achieve consistency and accuracy across the organization.
- *Lowering Operational Risk:* Delay in financial closing, not meeting deadlines for payment release, or making decisions based on incomplete/inaccurate information are some of the errors that lead to operational risks. To overcome this challenge, CFOs adopt RPA best practices, which reduce financial risks.
- *Improving Customer Satisfaction:* Banking, financial services, and insurance (BFSI) is a pivotal and hectic sector where companies deal with lengthy processes of servicing financial products and services and implementing various productive strategies to enhance the welfare of customers. RPA is growing in popularity because it can reduce costs, streamline processing, and drive better customer experiences. RPA offers many advantages for your customers. For example, with robots working alongside employees, customers can expect quicker response times.
- *Staff Freedom:* There is the indirect benefit of employee freedom. By taking care of laborious tasks, RPA gives your human customer service agents the time to manage more

complex customer issues. They can focus on providing excellent personal responses for better customer satisfaction.

Some of these benefits are illustrated in Figure 4.8 [5].

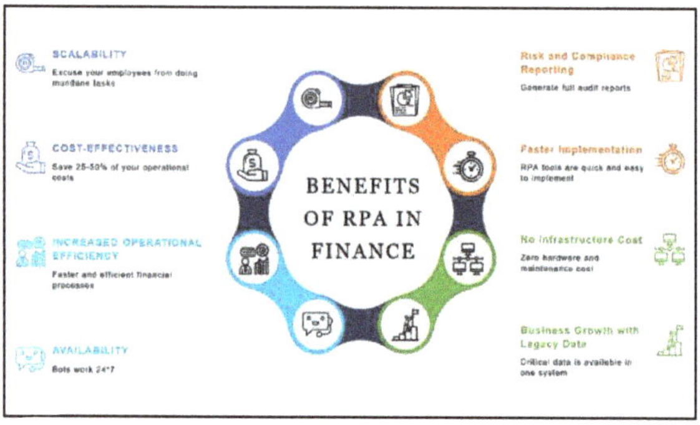

Figure 4.8 Some of the benefits of RPA [5].

4.5 Challenges

Modern technologies have modern challenges, and RPA is no exception. While RPA is not without its challenges, many of these can be overcome with proper preparation. RPA requires considerable training, governance, and implementation know-how. Businesses recognize RPA's potential to overcome some of their biggest challenges, including governance, compliance, reconciliation, and strategic planning. A major problem with monotonous tasks is that they destroy the mental health of the workers. Other challenges include the following [14]:

- *Implementation Challenges:* Implementing RPA comes with its challenges, including resistance from employees and integration complexities. Despite the potential, automation has been more difficult to implement in banking and finance than in other industries because a high amount of human intervention has been required to secure accounts and transfers. We tackle the challenges by ensuring clear communication about the benefits of RPA and involving employees in the transition process. Additionally, we continuously monitor and optimize the RPA system to handle increased loads and adapt to regulatory changes.

- *Privacy:* Bots can work with personally identifiable information governed by privacy requirements. Teams need to ensure this data is processed in conformance with local data protection laws such as the General Data Protection Regulation (GDPR). For example, if an RPA bot moved data outside of a given country without encryption, that would be a GDPR violation.
- *Security:* A major problem for all technologies centered around computers is their long-term security. Paper-based approaches are slow and require more effort to preserve the information. RPA bots sometimes need to access sensitive information to complete their tasks. If they are compromised, they pose an additional security risk for organizations.
- *Integration Complexity*: Integrating RPA with legacy financial systems and ensuring seamless interoperability poses a significant technical challenge.
- *Governance:* Companies should have strong governance in place to establish proper financial controls and accountability across all areas of the business. RPA bots help businesses maintain solid governance and ensure compliance by automating these tasks and performing the work more accurately than humans.

- *Unrealistic Expectations:* RPA is impactful but not a magic solution for all issues; one must set realistic goals and align with business objectives. Know what RPA can do and cannot do. Not all processes suit automation. To fully leverage this promising technology, companies need to understand what it is, recognize its benefits, and then decide when the best time is to implement it.
- *Change Management:* The introduction of RPA can evoke resistance from employees who fear job displacement. If you fail to explain the essence of the RPA change, massive protests against the technology (mostly covert) are inevitable. The goal is to show that the RPA tools are about automating routine tasks to free up time for more valuable, strategic work. Effective change management is crucial to mitigate this negativity.
- *Ensuring Compliance:* Adhering to stringent regulatory requirements while implementing RPA in finance demands meticulous attention to compliance standards and data security protocols. RPA offers the opportunity to enhance accuracy in financial processes while ensuring compliance with regulatory standards through consistent rule-based execution. Financial institutions are subject to stringent regulatory requirements that are continually evolving. Implementing RPA while maintaining compliance is an ongoing challenge. It requires monitoring and adapting automated processes to ensure they align with the latest regulatory changes, minimizing the risk of non-compliance and associated penalties. RPA can be used to automate compliance-related tasks such as KYC (know your customer) checks, AML (anti-money laundering) checks, and regulatory reporting.

- *Scalability:* As businesses grow, RPA solutions must adapt. Ensuring the scalability of RPA implementations is challenging, particularly when considering factors like increased transaction volumes, additional processes, and expanding service offerings. A well-defined scalability strategy is essential to accommodate growth without disrupting operations.
- *Maintenance:* RPA systems, like any technology, require regular maintenance and monitoring. Ensuring that bots operate effectively, handle exceptions, and remain up-to-date with process changes demands dedicated resources. Maintenance includes addressing issues, updating scripts, and optimizing bot performance.

Some of these challenges of RPA are displayed in Figure 4.9 [5].

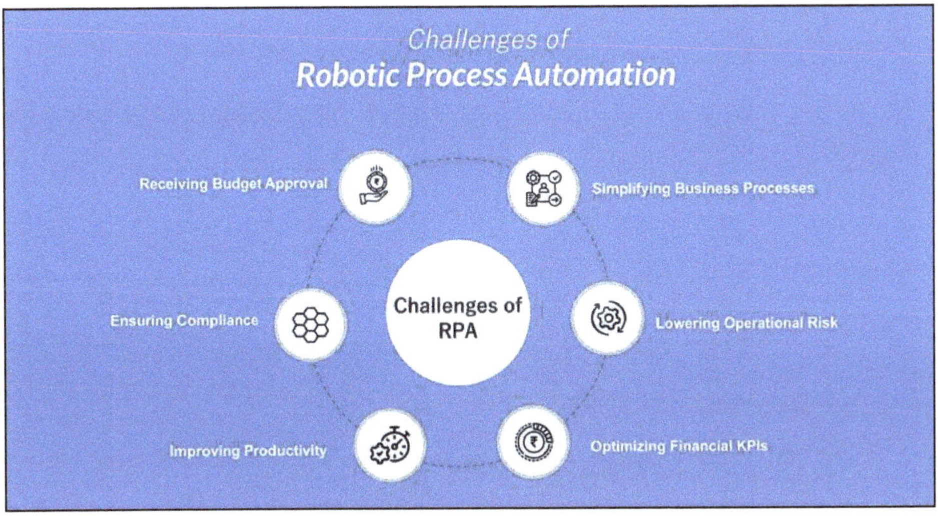

Figure 4.9 Some of the challenges of RPA [5].

4.6 Conclusion

Robotic process automation (RPA) refers to the software technology (bots) that are able to mimic human behavior and actions to complete tasks. It can help finance and accounting teams to improve efficiency, accuracy, compliance, and customer satisfaction. The emerging field of RPA in finance is proving to be a real game-changer for finance professionals. Instead of being chained to spreadsheets all day, RPA lets them complete tedious tasks in a fraction of the time it usually takes. RPA plays an important role in automating manual and time-consuming finance-related tasks. If implemented properly, RPA can prove revolutionary for the finance sector. As the technology expands and matures, adopting RPA will become a necessity for organizations looking to remain relevant and competitive in the fast-changing public accounting sector. RPA is now being incorporated in the accounting curriculum [15]. Looking ahead, the future of RPA in finance is promising. More information about robotic process automation in the financial services can be found in the books [16-28] and the following related journals:

- *International Journal of Finance*
- *The CPA Journal*

References

[1] "Robotic process automation in finance and accounting," May 2024,

https://www.solvexia.com/blog/rpa-in-finance-and-accounting

[2] A. S. Gillis and G. Lawton, "Robotic process automation (RPA),"

https://www.techtarget.com/searchcio/definition/RPA

[3] M. N. O. Sadiku, P. A. Adekunte, and J. O. Sadiku, "Robotic process automation in finance," *International Journal of Trend in Scientific Research and Development*, vol. 9, no. 2, March-April 2025, pp. 1269-1278.

[4] A. Raval, "Guidelines for implementing robotic process automation (RPA), from Gururaj Rao, Mahindra Finance, January 2020.

https://www.expresscomputer.in/news/guidelines-for-implementing-robotic-process-automation-rpa-from-gururaj-rao-mahindra-finance/45910/

[5] F. Caltin, "RPA in finance," February 2020,

https://www.plutushealthinc.com/post/rpa-in-finance

[6] S. Donnelly, "5 Benefits of robotic process automation in finance," September 2022,

https://www.financealliance.io/5-benefits-of-robotic-process-automation-in-finance/

[7] "Absolutely everything you need to know about robotic process automation,"

https://www.blueprism.com/guides/robotic-process-automation-rpa/

[8] "Robotic process automation in finance," September 2023,

https://kmbs.konicaminolta.us/blog/robotic-process-automation-in-finance/

[9] "Robotic process automation in finance,"

https://planergy.com/blog/robotic-process-automation-finance/

[10] "Robotics process automation in finance," September 2024,

https://www.apptunix.com/blog/robotics-process-automation-in-finance/

[11] "All about RPA in finance and banking,"

https://www.1rivet.com/insights/rpa-finance

[12] B. Blaney, "What is robotic accounting?" March 2025,

https://tipalti.com/resources/learn/robotic-accounting/

[13] S. Singh, "Robotic process automation in accounting: A comprehensive guide," September 2024,

https://savantlabs.io/blog/robotic-accounting/

[14] J. Barenz, "The future of finance: How RPA is reshaping financial processes,"

September 2024,

https://www.bakertilly.com/insights/rpa-reshaping-financial-processes

[15] M. Coe and N. Schwartz, "Robotic process automation in accounting education," October 2021,

https://www.cpajournal.com/2021/10/08/robotic-process-automation-in-accounting-education/

[16] J. S. Pimentel, *Robotic Process Automation in Finance: Concise Guide.* Staten House, 2024,

[17] N. Wilkins, *Robotics: What Beginners Need to Know about Robotic Process Automation, Mobile Robots, Artificial Intelligence, Machine Learning, Autonomous Vehicles, Speech Recognition, Drones, and Our Future.* Independently Published, 2019.

[18] G. Blokdyk, *The Operational Excellence Library; Mastering Robotic Process Automation (RPA) in Finance*. 5STARCooks, 2024.

[19] M. Smeets, R. Erhard, and T. Kaußler, *Robotic Process Automation (RPA) in the Financial Sector: Technology - Implementation - Success For Decision Makers and Users.* Springer, 2021.

[20] A. Javed et al., *Robotic Process Automation using UiPath StudioX: A Citizen Developer's Guide to Hyperautomation.* Apress, 2021.

[21] A. M. Tripathi, *Learning Robotic Process Automation: Create Software robots and automate business processes with the leading RPA tool – UiPath.* Packt Publishing, 2018.

[22] M. R. Smeets, A. Freßmann, and R. J. Ostendorf, *Robotic Process Automation in Use: Strategic Orientation - Practical Implementation - Audit-Proof Implementation.* Springer, 2024.

[23] T. Taulli, *The Robotic Process Automation Handbook: A Guide to Implementing RPA Systems.* Apress, 2020.

[24] R. Murdoch, *Robotic Process Automation: Guide To Building Software Robots, Automate Repetitive Tasks & Become An RPA Consultant*. Independently Published, 2018.

[25] D. Jenkins, *Automation in Finance: Mastering Financial Automation with AI, RPA, and Data-Driven Strategies for Modern Finance Professionals*. Independently Published, 2024.

[26] K. Wibbenmeyer, *The Simple Implementation Guide to Robotic Process Automation (RPA): How to Best Implement RPA in an Organization.* iUniverse, 2018.

[27] A. C. Tatto, *Financial Robotics: Automating Financial Operations*. Independently Published, 2025.

[28] M. Lacity and L. Willcocks, *Robotic Process and Cognitive Automation: The Next Phase.* Steve Brookes Publishing, 2018.

CHAPTER 5
ROBOTIC PROCESS AUTOMATION IN MARKETING

"When dealing with people, remember you are not dealing with creatures of logic, but creatures of emotion."
Dale Carnegie.

5.1 Introduction

In the ever-evolving digital landscape, businesses are constantly seeking innovative solutions to streamline operations, enhance productivity, and gain a competitive edge. One such transformative technology that has emerged as a game-changer is Robotic Process Automation (RPA). RPA uses software-based virtual bots to automate repetitive or labor-intensive tasks with high accuracy and speed. RPA is radically transforming the marketing industry. From automated price adjustments to competitor monitoring and data management, RPA is proving to be an invaluable ally in the marketing field. The adoption of RPA in marketing operations represents a significant shift towards enhancing efficiency, accuracy, and strategic decision-making, ultimately transforming how marketing departments function and deliver value.

Employees spend one-third of their time on routine administrative tasks rather than the skilled work they were hired to do. Robotic process automation (RPA) can help address this imbalance. The core of RPA is simple: Software-based robots mimic common human actions such as completing tables, filling out forms, or using applications. But they are not robots in the physical sense of the word. They are considered robotic because they can be programmed to take specific actions. RPA, or software robot, is a virtual system that helps to automate repetitive manual computing or business process tasks. RPA robots use user interfaces and application programming interfaces (API) to capture and scrape data and use applications as humans do. RPA lets your business gather more data, more quickly, and do so from any source. Properly applied, it can transform business operations [1].

Robotic process automation (RPA) refers to the use of software robots to automate highly repetitive and routine tasks that were traditionally performed by humans. It has emerged as a groundbreaking technology with the potential to revolutionize various operational facets of organizations, including marketing. This cutting-edge approach to automation is revolutionizing the way organizations execute their processes, ushering in a new era of efficiency and operational excellence. By using this transformative technology, organizations can boost operational efficiency, increase accuracy, and foster innovation, setting themselves up for long-term success in a constantly evolving market. By automating repetitive tasks, RPA enables marketing teams to focus on more strategic and creative efforts [2].

This chapter investigates the adoption of RPA in marketing operations, exploring its impact on efficiency, data accuracy, and overall effectiveness. It begins by explaining robotic process automation (RPA). It covers RPA in marketing and provides some of its applications. It highlights the benefits and challenges of RPA in marketing. It predicts the future of RPA in marketing. The last section concludes with comments.

5.2 What Is Robotic Process Automation?

Among the various forms of artificial intelligence, RPA stands out for its potential to significantly increase workforce productivity by reducing or eliminating the need to do repetitive tasks manually. Popular applications of RPA include data entry, data reconciliation, spreadsheet manipulation, systems integration, automated data reporting, analytics, email notifications, acquisitions, administrative services, finance, human resources, mission assurance, strategic communications, travel reimbursements, claims processing, and customer outreach and communications. These are just a few examples of the ways RPA is being used to remove the burden of manual, repetitive, and duplicative tasks from public service workers [3].

Robotic process automation is a form of automation software. It is a technology that can automate repetitive, rules-based tasks. Like an Excel macro operating within a spreadsheet, RPA can record actions performed across a personal computer, access systems, and perform specific tasks for human users. It uses software robots, more commonly called "bots," that mimic basic human-computer interactions. Figure 5.1 shows the symbol of RPA [4], while Figure 5.2 shows processes that RPA can automate [5]. Most industries use RPA. The government does too. Due to the repetitive nature of some tasks, the probability of human error increases. One way to eliminate errors is by using RPA.

Figure 5.1 Symbol of RPA [4].

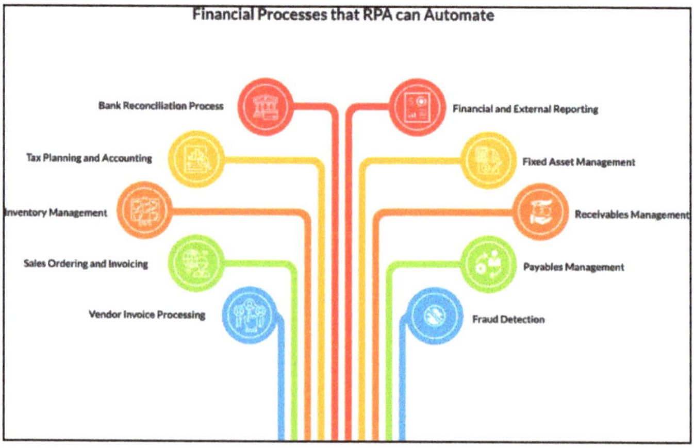

Figure 5.2 Processes that RPA can automate [5].

Robotic process automation solutions fall into three key categories: attended RPA, unattended RPA, and hybrid RPA, as shown in Figure 5.3 [6].

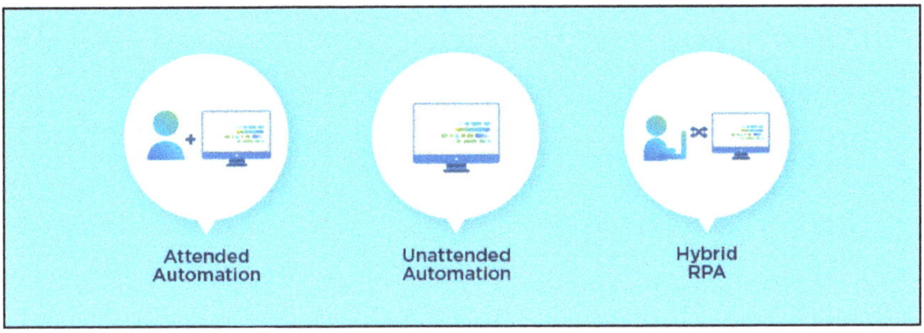

Figure 5.3 Three key categories of RPA [6].

Robotic process automation is a type of software that mimics the activity of a human being in carrying out a task within a process. It is a technology that automates repetitive tasks using software robots. RPA uses a set of automation tools to automate repetitive tasks and manual processes performed electronically. Since RPA can automate tasks that are rule-based, manual, repetitive, and tedious, delivering the highest levels of accuracy and eradicating human errors, it is a seamless fit for the finance industry. Here are some specific examples of what RPA in finance can do [7]:

- Opening emails and joining attachments
- Automatically logging into various applications on the web
- Shifting folders and files
- Copying and pasting

- Completing forms
- Collecting data from databases and the web
- Making calculations
- Connecting to system API
- Extracting structured data from documents
- Gathering stats from social media
- Following if/then decisions and rules

Some of these tasks are displayed in Figure 5.4 [6].

Figure 5.4 Some tasks RPA can perform [6].

At its core, robotic process automation (RPA) is a tool designed to mimic rule-based business processes, performing them seamlessly and without fatigue. RPA is a rule-driven method that is limited in its application. The technology functions much like a Microsoft Excel macro; the key difference is in power and reach. It follows set rules, similar to how an Excel macro works, to do things like move files or log into accounts. Growing as a popular solution in finance and accounting, RPA refers to software technology or "software robots" with artificial intelligence (AI) and machine learning (ML) capabilities. The "software robots" have the ability to learn and complete a high

volume of rules-based, repetitive tasks and business processes. They have the capacity to operate much faster than humans, with 100% precision and reliability, working around the clock.

Finance and human resources are just two examples of departments likely to have many use cases that RPA can help solve. Some examples of good use cases for RPA in finance include processing customer orders, ensuring timely vendor payments, and managing period-end financial close processes. For human resources, some examples include employee onboarding, time tracking, and leave of absence management. Processes where human judgment is needed are not appropriate for RPA since RPA automations rely on clear, consistently applied rules [8].

Along with RPA, one should be aware of both business process automation (BPA) and digital process automation (DPA) – two commonly used automation technologies that robotics process automation can be paired with to optimize and streamline a digital transformation. BPA refers to the use of technology to automate complex, multi-step workflows, typically very specific to a company's core business functions. DPA offers dual power by automating processes from end to end and optimizing common workflows that involve external human interactions (i.e., sales, management). Separately, RPA and AI are quite powerful, but leveraging them together is undoubtedly advantageous to any financial institution. When deployed together, AI is the "brains" behind RPA's bots [9].

5.3 Robotic Process Automation In Marketing

Robotic process automation (RPA) is an advanced tool of technology that makes it easy to develop, deploy, and control software bots that mimic human activities and communicate with digital systems and software. It uses software-based robots to automate business processes and reduce error risks. RPA in marketing automates repetitive, rule-based tasks like data entry, reporting, and campaign setup, freeing marketers for strategic work, increasing accuracy, and improving efficiency. RPA marks a significant change in business automation, providing a powerful way to enhance workflows, lower costs, and create new growth and innovation opportunities.

There is now a rapidly growing interest among marketing professionals towards prioritizing automation as a strategic imperative. Software robots are now driving innovation across marketing organizations. Traditionally, marketing tasks were manual, labor-intensive, and prone to human error. As marketing strategies became more sophisticated, incorporating elements such as multi-channel campaigns, real-time analytics, and personalized customer engagement, the complexity of marketing operations increased correspondingly. RPA, as a technology, is designed to automate repetitive, rule-based tasks typically performed by human employees. The application of RPA in marketing operations encompasses a wide range of activities, from automating data entry and report generation to streamlining customer interactions and campaign management. RPA not only improves productivity but also reduces the risk of errors associated with manual processes. As RPA takes over repetitive tasks, marketing teams may need to adapt by focusing on higher-value activities that require human judgment, creativity, and strategic thinking. Figure 5.5 shows how RPA is used in nine industries, including marketing [10].

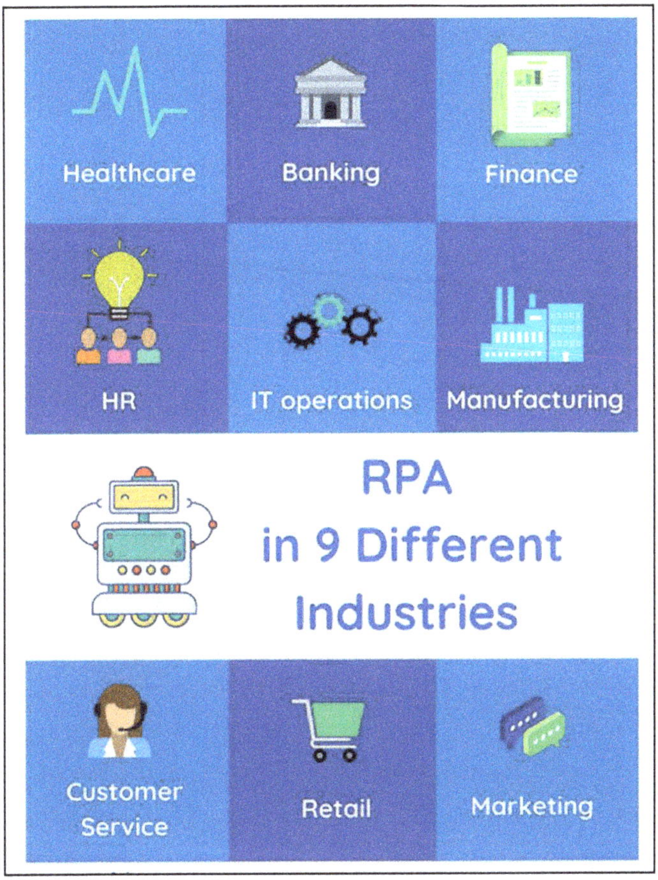

Figure 5.5 How RPA is used in nine industries, including marketing [10].

5.4 Applications Of Robotic Process Automation In Marketing

Robotic process automation (RPA) is utilized widely across various industries and business functions because of its ability to streamline processes and increase efficiency. Common applications include automated pay-per-click (PPC) bid adjustments, competitor price monitoring, lead data entry, content scheduling, and customer data management, all leading to cost savings, better resource allocation, and enhanced customer experiences. From pricing automation to marketing automation to data management, RPA is making marketing operations more efficient and effective. Key applications of RPA in marketing include the following [10-13]:

- *Finance and Banking:* Banking and financial institutions are investing in RPA to improve trading, compliance, internal controls, customer service levels, and error reduction. Financial institutions are leveraging RPA solutions to transform their business operations. Common applications include automating transaction processing, managing compliance reporting, and handling customer onboarding processes. RPA helps banks offer faster, more reliable services to their customers, boosting satisfaction and loyalty. From loan processing to report generation, RPA is streamlining routine processes for banking teams.
- *Retail:* Customers expect a faster shopping experience with an uncompromising attitude towards error. RPA in retail supports various activities such as inventory, supply chain, returns processing, invoice and contract management, and store

planning management. Retailers use RPA tools to enhance customer service, manage inventory, and streamline order processing. Bots can automatically update inventory levels, process returns, and handle customer inquiries in real-time, improving the shopping experience. Furthermore, RPA enables personalized marketing by analyzing customer data and tailoring promotions and recommendations to individual preferences. Reducing human intervention and human error in an online sales business will give the brand a competitive advantage. By automating these processes, retailers can significantly improve efficiency, reduce manual errors, cut operational costs, and free employees to focus on more strategic, customer-centric activities. Figure 5.6 shows some use cases of RPA in retail management [14].

Figure 5.6 Some use cases of RPA in retail management [14].

- *Advertising:* Robotic automation of processes and development reduces advertising costs in social networks by 50%. RPA is a great tool to automatically adjust bids for pay-per-click (PPC) ad campaigns for maximum impact. You can schedule when your Google Ads can go live and can increase bids when your target audience is inclined to make purchases. Marketing teams should not only focus on pricing, but also on understanding their competitors' advertising tactics. In modern advertising, visuals are elements of attraction.
- *E-commerce:* Many e-commerce companies struggle to effectively manage their products and keep inventory levels up to date. E-commerce retailers need to know what their inventory levels are at all times to ensure they have enough product to meet demand. RPA can streamline and expedite order tracking for you and your customers. Personalization can be a real game-changer for boosting e-commerce conversion rates. The modern online shopper wants their buying experience personalized. Figure 5.7 shows RPA use cases in e-commerce [15].

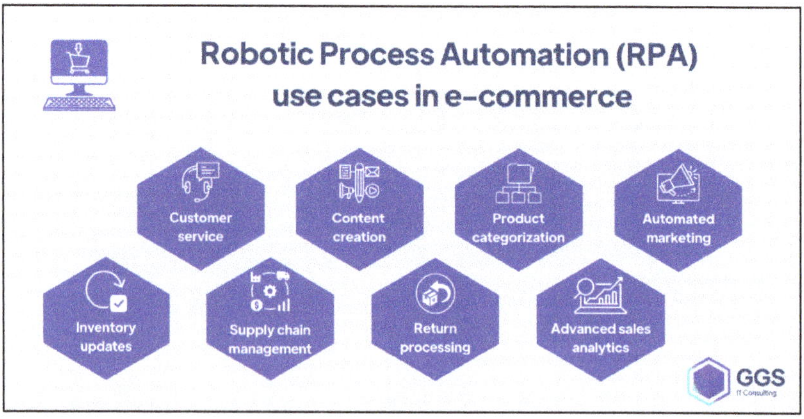

Figure 5.7 RPA use cases in e-commerce [15].

- *Customer Service:* Customer service is an essential part of every company. When customer service is not optimized, your company will likely see a negative impact. RPA can assist with routine tasks that take up too much time, allowing employees to focus on fostering better customer relationships. Customers will no longer need to wait for a representative to have their questions answered.
- *Human Resources:* The human resources (HR) industry handles more than its fair share of time-consuming tasks. With RPA, HR professionals can automate daily tasks such as sending out mass emails, updating data and records, onboarding team members, and managing payroll. For example, when a new employee is hired, HR is faced with onboarding tasks and paperwork that can take more time than they have in a day. Recruitment and onboarding, as well as performance management activities, are some of those experiences enhanced by the AI-RPA tool.
- *Marketing Automation:* This can take over the less glamorous, manual tasks, giving your marketing team the ability to use their expertise and creativity to grow your market share. Marketing automation can include monitoring as well as additional layers of security, such as encryption. It can notify you of anomalies when they occur. It also helps reduce access to information, put better controls in place, increase security, and provide compliance. RPA tools in the marketing department can take care of a multitude of tasks and provide insights and opportunities you would not otherwise have. For example, you can automate email campaigns, generate reports, and manage multiple channel communications. Figure 5.8 shows the benefits of marketing automation [16].

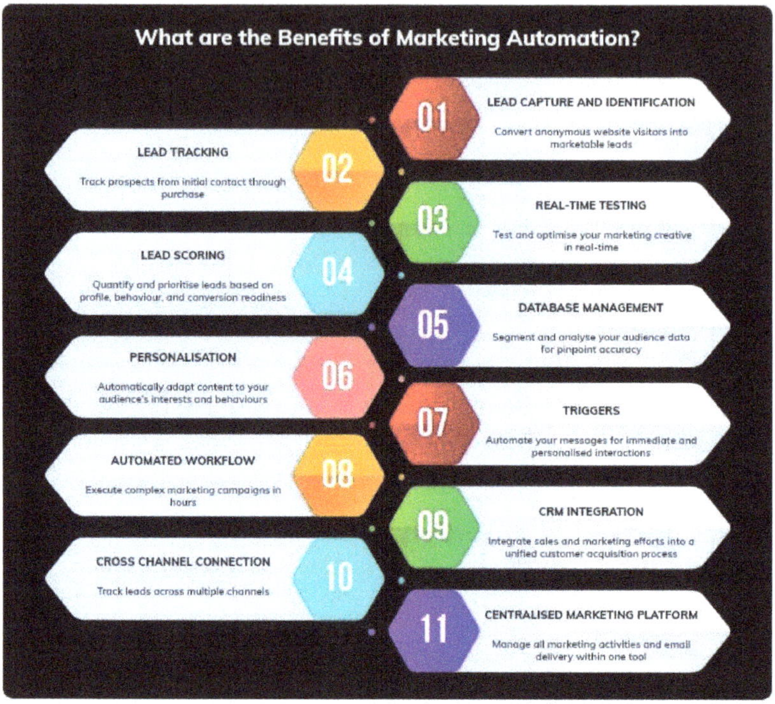

Figure 5.8 Some benefits of marketing automation [16].

- *Pricing Automation:* One of the primary applications of RPA in marketing is pricing automation. Setting competitive and accurate product prices is crucial for any business. RPA tools streamline this task by ensuring accuracy and competitiveness. By using processes such as Optical Character Recognition (OCR) and Natural Language Processing (NLP), they can automatically adjust prices within predefined margins. Beyond pricing, competitor monitoring has become a vital strategy for marketing teams. This practice allows companies to stay ahead of trends and respond effectively to market tactics. Marketing teams should not only focus on pricing, but also on understanding their competitors' advertising tactics.

- *Inventory Automation:* RPA automates critical inventory tasks, from tracking stock levels across multiple locations to processing purchase orders and updating product databases. Bots can monitor sales data, trigger reorders when stock is low, and reconcile discrepancies, ensuring optimal inventory levels. This reduces manual errors, minimizes stockouts, and enhances supply chain efficiency, improving product availability and customer satisfaction.
- *Data Management:* Collecting information from multiple sources and in different formats poses a significant difficulty for marketers when dealing with multiple portfolios of items. Data management has become an area where robotic process automation (RPA) is making a significant mark. RPA technology has revolutionized data processing by automating repetitive tasks, improving efficiency, and reducing errors. Integrated data management platforms with RPA are able to organize, analyze, and use this data effectively. Automating data management tasks frees marketing teams from manual entry, allowing them to focus on data interpretation.
- *Customer Service:* Customer service departments can integrate marketing and sales inquiries with the onboarding process to streamline the customer experience. They are also better able to maintain customer relationships with omnichannel solutions by including interactions and requests in CRM systems.
- *RPA-Powered Chatbots:* Conversational marketing plays a significant role in both B2B and B2C marketing strategies. A chatbot is a dialog program built on a template script: typical questions and answers, standard actions and reactions.

Combining artificial intelligence-powered chatbots with RPA technology can be highly effective in converting website visitors. When a visitor seeks certain information to aid in their decision-making process, the integrated RPA bot can quickly retrieve the requested information from various backend systems and databases, making it accessible to the visitor.

- *Financial Reporting:* For businesses that generate large volumes of financial data, RPA can automate the task of compiling and preparing reports. By automating data entry, calculation, and other tasks, RPA can help businesses reduce the time it takes to generate accurate financial reports. Robotic process automation (RPA) can be used to automate account reconciliation. RPA can be used to extract data from multiple sources, including accounting software, ERP systems, and databases.

5.5 Benefits

The adoption of RPA technology brings significant benefits to organizations, enhancing efficiency, accuracy, and reducing costs. RPA automates routine tasks, freeing up employees for higher-value work and improving scalability and compliance. These robots can replicate various human-user actions, including entering data, processing transactions, and communicating with other systems. By using software robots, companies can automate many repetitive, rule-based tasks. This frees up employees to concentrate on more strategic and valuable work. Other benefits of RPA in marketing include [12]:

- *Automation*: Business process automation in general, and robotic process automation in particular, offer several benefits across business functions. Robotic process automation is one element of a larger move towards automation. Businesses choosing to go the automation route can choose between using standalone robotic process automation or combining it with advanced business process automation capabilities that seek to optimize processes across the organization. If the task is consistent, repeatable, and has decision trees that always lead to a definite outcome, it can likely be automated via bots. Robotic process automation significantly reduces the number and frequency of errors in performing repetitive tasks. It also enables 24/7 task completion without the need for human intervention.
- *Increased Efficiency:* RPA achieves the unique feat of never making human mistakes and being available 24/7. RPA reduces the time required to carry out business tasks. RPA bots are incredibly efficient at handling repetitive tasks that traditionally require human intervention. By automating these processes, businesses can achieve tasks faster and with consistent output 24/7, thus significantly speeding up overall workflow. The implementation of RPA reduces the potential for errors in tasks.
- *Enhanced Customer Satisfaction*: Perhaps, the most exciting benefit from RPA in marketing is the application of machine learning on the marketing funnel and customer experience. Rules-based decisions in our workflow can be improved by becoming experience-based over time. Today, marketers want to be more directly involved in customer engagement. Through AI marketing automation, companies create highly targeted marketing initiatives, send emails, and analyze

customer information. It helps in achieving improved customer satisfaction through products such as chatbots and sentiment analysis.

- *Better Employee Morale:* RPA workforce automation tools can help improve the human work experience. Instead of being tasked with data entry, employees can spend their time focused on more strategic and creative work. RPA also opens the door for staff reskilling and upskilling. With automated scripts handling manual tasks, businesses can bring employees up to speed with training in responsible AI use.
- *Better Decision-Making:* In today's digital environment, businesses rely on data-driven decisions to help various core processes in achieving their targets. Nowhere is this more important than in marketing processes where teams work swiftly and unearth actionable insights from piles of data to craft relevant strategies to stay ahead of the competition. The bottleneck in this process is the human factor; it can take an extremely long time to manually analyze all the available data before being able to make accurate business decisions. RPA for digital marketing can result in an extremely agile marketing department by automating the tedious process of turning big data into applicable marketing recommendations.
- *Cost Savings:* Implementing RPA can lead to substantial cost reductions. Reduction in the time and effort required to complete labor-intensive processes means less money spent on these processes. RPA lowers labor costs and the need for additional headcount for repetitive work. By automating routine tasks, companies can reduce the need for additional personnel and minimize human error, which can be costly. Over time, these savings can be significant, allowing businesses to allocate resources to more critical areas.

- *Improved Accuracy:* Human error is a common issue in manual processes, but RPA offers a solution by executing predefined tasks with high precision. This accuracy is particularly valuable in industries where even a minor mistake can have serious repercussions, such as finance and healthcare.
- *Scalability:* One of the standout features of RPA is its scalability. RPA easily handles peak demand and growth without linear increases in staffing. Businesses can easily scale their automation efforts up or down based on current needs without a corresponding increase in errors or costs. As business requirements change or volumes increase, RPA systems can be easily adjusted, scaled up, or scaled down, thereby providing a highly flexible solution to meet evolving business demands.
- *Flexibility:* Unlike traditional automation methods, RPA seamlessly integrates with existing systems and applications, eliminating the need for extensive system modifications or costly infrastructure overhauls. This agility and flexibility make RPA a highly attractive solution for businesses seeking to optimize their operations without disrupting their existing technology landscape. This flexibility is crucial for businesses looking to grow or adapt to seasonal market fluctuations.

Some benefits of RPA are depicted in Figure 5.9 [17].

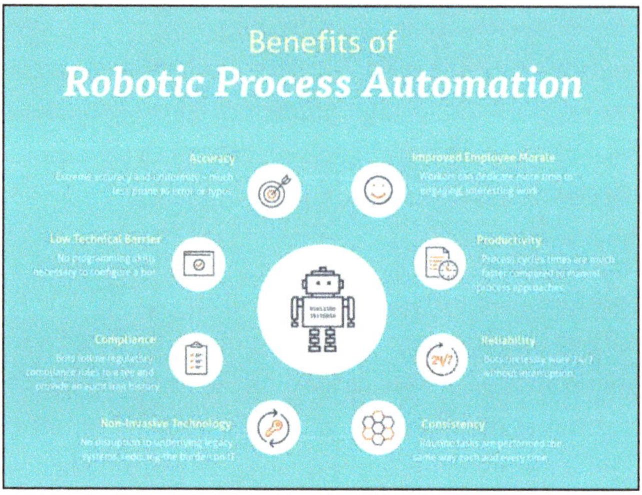

Figure 5.9 Some benefits of RPA [17].

5.6 Challenges

Although RPA offers significant advantages for organizations, it comes with several potential challenges and key considerations. These include identifying processes for workforce automation, managing data quality and integration, navigating ethical governance concerns, and addressing scalability and maintenance needs. One of the primary concerns is the potential impact on the workforce. Not every process is a good fit for automation. RPA may not be the best fit for a particular application. Organizations may also encounter resistance to change from employees who are accustomed to traditional methods of working. Other challenges of RPA in marketing include the following [1,12,18]:

- *Ethical Concerns:* Ethical and regulatory considerations play a crucial role in the adoption process of RPA. RPA can introduce concerns around ethical data use. For example, if companies lack visibility into what data is being collected and how it is being used, the effect could be compliance or legal challenges. Workforce implications, including the potential displacement of certain job roles and the need for reskilling, require careful consideration and proactive management. Ensuring that RPA implementations adhere to legal and ethical standards is crucial for maintaining trust and protecting organizational reputation.
- *Compliance:* As with any technology that involves data processing and automation, organizations must ensure compliance with data protection regulations and ethical standards. Marketing teams often deal with a wealth of personal data. This requires companies, IT departments, and marketing teams to follow many laws, rules, and regulations. In the event of audits or compliance evaluations, organizations must be able to show where data was captured, how it was obtained, and what changes it has undergone. Failure to demonstrate this transparency could result in fines or sanctions.
- *Security and Privacy:* RPA tools may also introduce potential privacy and security risks. Working with internal, lead, and customer data along with multiple programs and processes requires additional security and privacy considerations. RPA implementations must be designed with privacy and security considerations in mind to protect sensitive customer information and maintain trust. This includes implementing robust data governance practices and ensuring transparency in how data is handled and processed by RPA systems. Ensuring

data privacy and complying with data protection regulations are essential to maintaining customer trust and upholding ethical standards.

- *Integration:* The first obstacle often encountered is ensuring that existing systems can seamlessly integrate with RPA software. Effective RPA depends on high-quality data and the ability to integrate this data across legacy systems and modern applications. Legacy systems and modern architectures are distinctly different; what works for one may not work for another. Legacy systems may not work with modern APIs, but still contain critical operational data. Because these solutions automate manual processes typically handled by humans, they are capable of finding and extracting key data from disparate and disconnected solutions.
- *Workforce:* Another primary concern is the impact of RPA on the workforce. The automation of routine tasks can lead to job displacement, particularly for roles that were previously involved in manual processes. This shift necessitates the reskilling and upskilling of employees to prepare them for new roles that focus on strategic and value-added activities. Organizations must proactively address these workforce implications by investing in training programs and providing support for employees during the transition.

5.7 Future Of Robotic Process Automation In Marketing

In the field of marketing, robotic process automation (RPA) has emerged as a transformative force, streamlining complex processes and enabling marketers to refocus their efforts on strategy and creativity.

Software robots, or RPA, will be a fundamental part of innovation in marketing. The field of RPA is rapidly evolving, with exciting advancements on the horizon. The future of RPA in marketing operations holds significant potential for further innovation and growth. It is poised for continued innovation, driven by advancements in technology and evolving industry needs. Emerging technologies, such as artificial intelligence, machine learning, big data, and blockchain, are expected to enhance the capabilities of RPA systems, enabling more sophisticated automation and data analysis.

Looking to the future, the integration of artificial intelligence with RPA holds great promise for further enhancing automation capabilities. The integration promises to deliver deeper insights and more personalized marketing experiences, further advancing the effectiveness of marketing operations. It has expanded the capabilities of automation systems, enabling advanced data analysis and predictive modeling. Figure 5.10 shows how to enhance RPA with AI [19]. Any company that implements AI-enhancing RPA solutions in today's market will prepare for competitiveness in a market dominated by technology. Similarly, the integration of RPA with blockchain technology can enhance transparency and traceability in marketing operations, particularly in areas such as supply chain management and fraud prevention [18]. RPA is poised to completely revolutionize the business world as we know it. It is important for businesses of all sizes to get on board now and start preparing for the future of marketing.

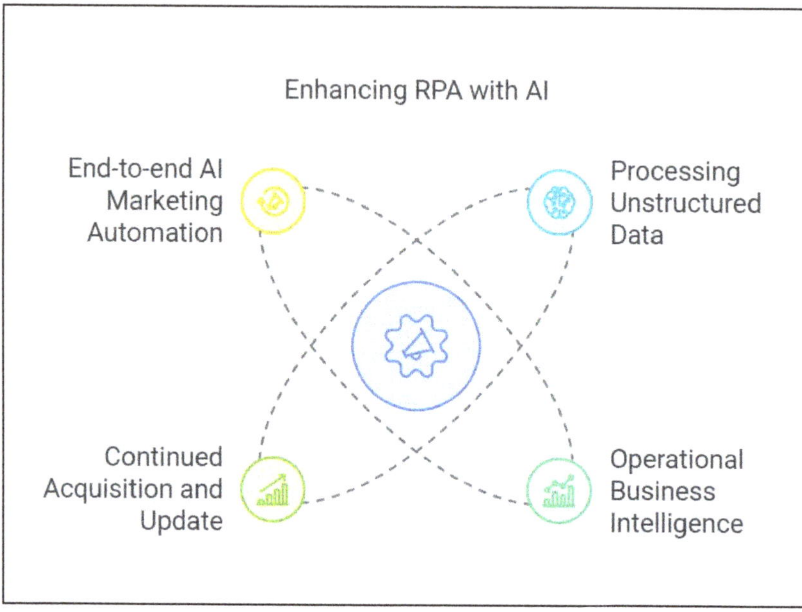

Figure 5.10 How to enhance RPA with AI [19].

5.8 Conclusion

Robotic process automation (RPA) is one of the forms of business process automation that strives to imitate human actions associated with digital systems. It is increasingly being integrated into various business functions, including marketing operations, due to its potential to enhance efficiency and effectiveness. The adoption of RPA in marketing operations represents a transformative development that has the potential to enhance efficiency, accuracy, and strategic decision-making. RPA is a powerful tool that can help businesses to streamline their marketing efforts and improve efficiency. By automating tasks, businesses can free up time for more important work, improve accuracy, and enhance the customer experience. RPA is designed to take over repetitive digital tasks. These include compiling data from various sources and applications, organizing and analyzing it, and taking prearranged actions based on the outcome [20].

Although RPA has gained a lot of attention from industry analysts, its use in marketing is currently limited. The future of RPA in marketing appears to be very promising, with many experts predicting that the technology will continue to grow and evolve in the coming years. Its integration with emerging technologies like AI/ML, AR/VR, big data, etc., will surely solve complex issues and speed up business processes with utmost efficiency. As RPA becomes more sophisticated, marketers will likely be able to automate even more complex processes, improving efficiency and reducing costs even further [4]. More information about robotic process automation in marketing can be found in the books [21-23].

References

[1] "What is RPA (robotic process automation)?"https://www.salesforce.com/artificial-intelligence/rpa-robotic-process-automation/

[2] M. N. O. Sadiku and J. O. Sadiku, "Robotic process automation in marketing," *International Journal of Trend in Scientific Research and Development,* vol. 10, no. 1, January-February 2026, pp. 279-290.

[3] N. Komitsky, "Putting robotic process automation to work in the federal government,"

https://www.managementconcepts.com/resource/putting-robotic-process-automation-to-work-in-the-federal-government/

[4] "What is robotic process automation (RPA)? How does it work?" February 2023,

https://solidpro-es.com/what-is-robotic-process-automation-rpa-how-it-works/

[5] F. Caltin, "RPA in finance," February 2020,

https://www.plutushealthinc.com/post/rpa-in-finance

[6] "Absolutely everything you need to know about robotic process automation,"

https://www.blueprism.com/guides/robotic-process-automation-rpa/

[7] S. Donnelly, “5 Benefits of robotic process automation in finance,” September 2022,

https://www.financealliance.io/5-benefits-of-robotic-process-automation-in-finance/

[8] “Robotic process automation in finance,” September 2023,

https://kmbs.konicaminolta.us/blog/robotic-process-automation-in-finance/

[9] “Robotic process automation in finance,”

https://planergy.com/blog/robotic-process-automation-finance/

[10] “RPA examples and use cases in 9 different industries,” November 2021,

https://www.comidor.com/blog/rpa/rpa-use-cases/

[11] “Unleashing efficiency: The power of robotic process automation (RPA) in business,”

https://www.fujifilm.com/fbhk/en/solutions/insights/article/unleashing-efficiency-rpa-in-business

[12] “What is marketing automation and why do businesses need it?”

https://www.automationanywhere.com/solutions/sales-and-marketing/rpa-in-marketing

[13] “The RPA revolution in the marketing industry: A glimpse into the future,”

https://www.digital-robots.com/en/news/the-rpa-revolution-in-the-marketing-industry-a-glimpse-of-the-future

[14] “RPA in retail: Top 11 use cases that are transforming the industry,”

https://marutitech.com/rpa-in-retail/

[15] M. Tajak, “How robotic process automation is changing the world of e-commerce,” January 2022,

https://ggsitc.com/blog/how-robotic-process-automation-is-changing-the-world-of-e-commerce

[16] H. Mansuriya, “Implementing RPA in marketing strategies,” January 2024,

https://spaculus.com/blog/rpa-marketing-strategy/

[17] “What is robotic process automation (RPA)?” January 2022,

https://7wdata.be/predictive-analytics/what-is-robotic-process-automation-rpa/

[18] G. Wilson, O. Johnson, and W. Brown, “The adoption of robotic process automation in marketing operations,” August 2024,

https://www.preprints.org/manuscript/202408.0327

[19] I. Sharma, “The role of AI in enhancing robotic process automation,” May 2025,

https://valueinnovationlabs.com/blog/robotic-process-automation/the-role-of-ai-in-enhancing-robotic-process-automation/

[20] N. Arant, "The upside of robotic process automation in your marketing strategy," January 2023,

https://www.sparkhound.com/blog/the-upside-of-robotic-process-automation-in-your-marketing-strategy/

[21] C. Juarez, *Unleashing Efficiency: The Power of Robotic Process Automation (RPA).* Independently Published, 2023.

[22] H. Mahey, *Robotic Process Automation with Automation Anywhere: Techniques to Fuel Business Productivity And Intelligent Automation Using RPA.* Packt Publishing, 2020.

[23] T. Taulli, *The Robotic Process Automation Handbook: A Guide to Implementing RPA Systems.* Apress, 2020.

CHAPTER 6
ROBOTIC PROCESS AUTOMATION IN MANUFACTURING

"A pessimist sees the difficulty in every opportunity; an optimist sees the opportunity in every difficulty."
Winston Churchill.

6.1 Introduction

As the manufacturing industry grapples with ongoing labor shortages, high turnover rates, and increasing demand for skilled workers, companies are turning increasingly to innovative technologies. Robotic process automation (RPA) is emerging as a key solution to bridge the workforce gap and optimize efficiency and precision. The software executes a set of instructions to replicate tasks typically done by humans, enabling manufacturers to streamline operations, reduce costs, and minimize errors. Its impact on manufacturing is growing in several areas, including supply chain management, quality control, preventive maintenance, and administrative automation [1]. The manufacturing industry is expected to become a huge beneficiary of RPA technology due to the manual repetitive tasks that characterize traditional aspects of manufacturing. Figure 6.1 provides a definition of robotic process automation [2], while Figure 6.2 shows a typical manufacturing environment [3].

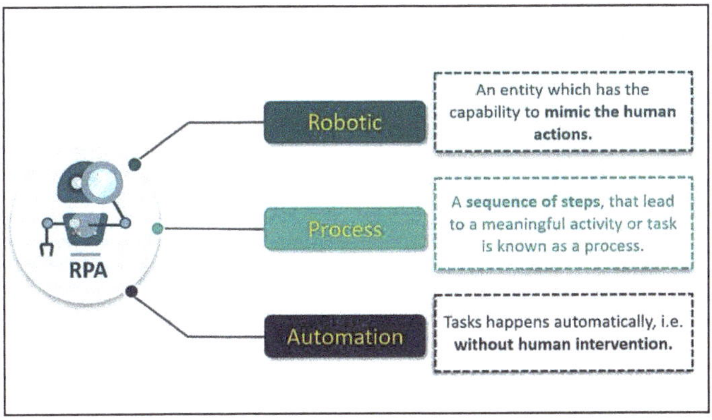

Figure 6.1 A definition of robotic process automation [2].

Figure 6.2 A typical manufacturing environment [3].

Robotic process automation (RPA) presents itself as a game-changing technology that enables manufacturers to boost efficiency, spur innovation, and automate monotonous operations. It is transforming the way organizations across different industries do business. It allows organizations to automate certain types of work processes to reduce the time spent on costly manual tasks and increase efforts to deliver mission-critical work. It eliminates the need for employees to perform repetitive tasks by integrating software that performs the same set of steps as the employee. One of the main differentiators of RPA from other solutions is that it performs tasks that do not require deep cognitive capabilities.

Robotic process automation (RPA) in manufacturing uses software bots to automate repetitive, rule-based digital tasks, improving efficiency and accuracy. It is a technology that manufacturing businesses use to automate high-volume, repeatable tasks. It is increasingly becoming a key component of manufacturing and warehousing environments because it is helping manufacturing organizations do more with less. RPA can help enable manufacturers to improve productivity, meet customers' expectations, and consistently drive product innovation—all while lowering costs. Manufacturers can integrate RPA bots on the production floor in addition to back-office operations. RPA in manufacturing is revolutionizing the way industrial operations are managed, optimized, and scaled [4].

In this chapter, we will discuss the role of RPA in the manufacturing industry. The chapter begins with explaining the concept of robotic process automation (RPA). It describes RPA in manufacturing and provides some of its applications. It highlights the benefits and challenges of RPA in manufacturing. It predicts the future of RPA in manufacturing. The last section concludes with comments.

6.2 What Is Robotic Process Automation?

Among the various forms of artificial intelligence, RPA stands out for its potential to significantly increase workforce productivity by reducing or eliminating the need to do repetitive tasks manually. Popular applications of RPA include data entry, data reconciliation, spreadsheet manipulation, systems integration, automated data reporting, analytics, email notifications, acquisitions, administrative services, finance, human resources, mission assurance, strategic communications, travel reimbursements, claims processing, and customer outreach and communications. These are just a few examples of the ways RPA is being used to remove the burden of manual, repetitive, and duplicative tasks from public service workers [5].

Robotic process automation is a form of automation software. It is a technology that can automate repetitive, rules-based tasks. Like an Excel macro operating within a spreadsheet, RPA can record actions performed across a personal computer, access systems, and perform specific tasks for human users. It uses software robots, more commonly called "bots," that mimic basic human-computer interactions. Figure 6.3 shows the symbol of RPA [6], while Figure 6.4 shows processes that RPA can automate [7]. Most industries use RPA. The government does too. Due to the repetitive nature of some tasks, the probability of human error increases. One way to eliminate errors is by using RPA.

Figure 6.3 Symbol of RPA [6].

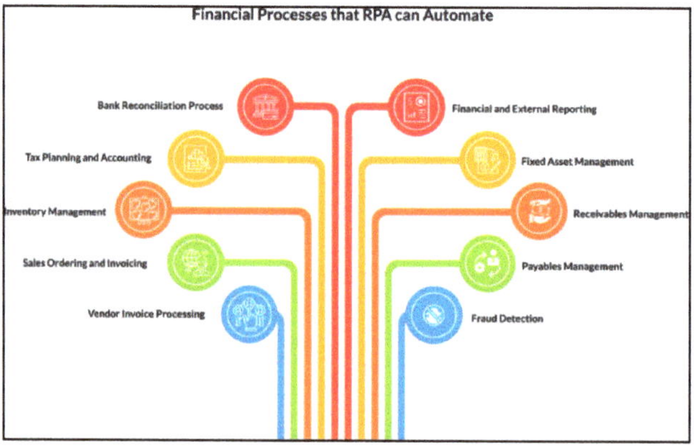

Figure 6.4 Processes that RPA can automate [7].

Robotic process automation solutions fall into three key categories: attended RPA, unattended RPA, and hybrid RPA, as shown in Figure 6.5 [8].

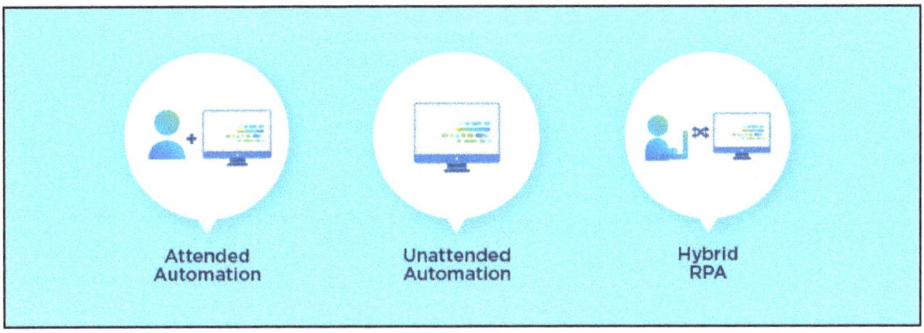

Figure 6.5 Three key categories of RPA [8].

Robotic process automation is a type of software that mimics the activity of a human being in carrying out a task within a process. It is a technology that automates repetitive tasks using software robots. RPA uses a set of automation tools to automate repetitive tasks and manual processes performed electronically. Since RPA can automate tasks that are rule-based, manual, repetitive, and tedious, delivering the highest levels of accuracy and eradicating human errors, it is a seamless fit for the finance industry. Here are some specific examples of what RPA in finance can do [9]:

- Opening emails and joining attachments
- Automatically logging into various applications on the web
- Shifting folders and files
- Copying and pasting

- Completing forms
- Collecting data from databases and the web
- Making calculations
- Connecting to system API
- Extracting structured data from documents
- Gathering stats from social media
- Following if/then decisions and rules

Some of these tasks are displayed in Figure 6.6 [8].

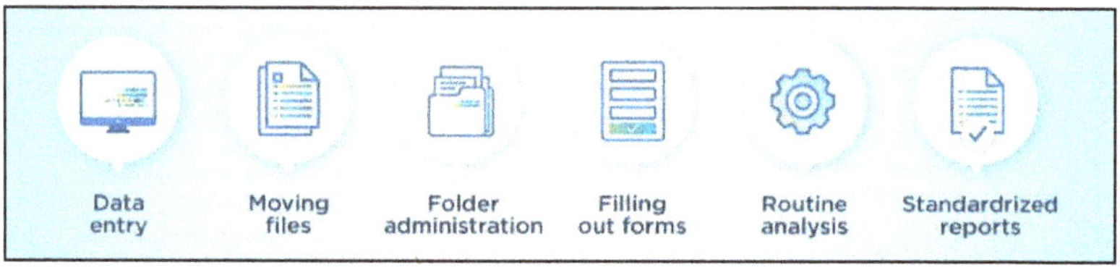

Figure 6.6 Some tasks RPA can perform [8].

At its core, robotic process automation (RPA) is a tool designed to mimic rule-based business processes, performing them seamlessly and without fatigue. RPA is a rule-driven method that is limited in its application. The technology functions much like a Microsoft Excel macro; the key difference is in power and reach. It follows set rules, similar to how an Excel macro works, to do things like move files or log into accounts. Growing as a popular solution in finance and accounting, RPA refers to software technology or "software robots" with artificial intelligence (AI) and machine learning (ML) capabilities. The "software robots" have the ability to learn and complete a high

volume of rules-based, repetitive tasks and business processes. They have the capacity to operate much faster than humans, with 100% precision and reliability, working around the clock.

Finance and human resources are just two examples of departments likely to have many use cases that RPA can help solve. Some examples of good use cases for RPA in finance include processing customer orders, ensuring timely vendor payments, and managing period-end financial close processes. For human resources, some examples include employee onboarding, time tracking, and leave of absence management. Processes where human judgment is needed are not appropriate for RPA since RPA automations rely on clear, consistently applied rules [10].

Along with RPA, one should be aware of both business process automation (BPA) and digital process automation (DPA) – two commonly used automation technologies that robotics process automation can be paired with to optimize and streamline a digital transformation. BPA refers to the use of technology to automate complex, multi-step workflows, typically very specific to a company's core business functions. DPA offers dual power by automating processes from end to end and optimizing common workflows that involve external human interactions (i.e., sales, management). Separately, RPA and AI are quite powerful, but leveraging them together is undoubtedly advantageous to any financial institution. When deployed together, AI is the "brains" behind RPA's bots [11].

6.3 Robotic Process Automation In Manufacturing

The manufacturing industry is one of the more complicated and labor-intensive industries. It is an ever-changing industry where technological advancements are reshaping operations and challenging traditional production models. Automation in the manufacturing sector has long outperformed manual processes in gathering relevant data, visualizing all critical production KPIs, and then delivering final reports to the right stakeholders. However, when compared to other industries like banking, financial services, insurance, and retail, the manufacturing industry has been slower to deploy software automation in core manufacturing processes of production, operations, and maintenance.

Before automation, a manufacturing company received hundreds of invoices from various suppliers each month. Employees manually input invoice data into the enterprise resource management (ERP) system, verify details, and process payments. Completing tasks manually is time-consuming, error-prone, and far from creative, yet vital to keeping the factory running. After automation, an RPA bot handles the end-to-end process in seconds. Bots do them all way faster and without lapses. RPA involves creating a set of instructions that guide the software robots to perform specific tasks.

Robotic process automation (RPA) has emerged as a transformative technology, offering significant advantages to manufacturers seeking to streamline operations, reduce costs, and improve overall productivity. It uses software robots to automate repetitive, rule-based tasks traditionally performed by humans. These tasks can range from data entry and processing to complex calculations and report generation. By automating repetitive and rule-based tasks, RPA significantly reduces the burden on human labor, allowing workers to focus on more strategic and value-added activities. With RPA in manufacturing, you bring the benefits of precision and speed to your human-powered workflow. By implementing RPA, manufacturers can automate routine processes and achieve faster, error-free, and consistent results. Figure 6.7 is a representation of RPA in manufacturing [12].

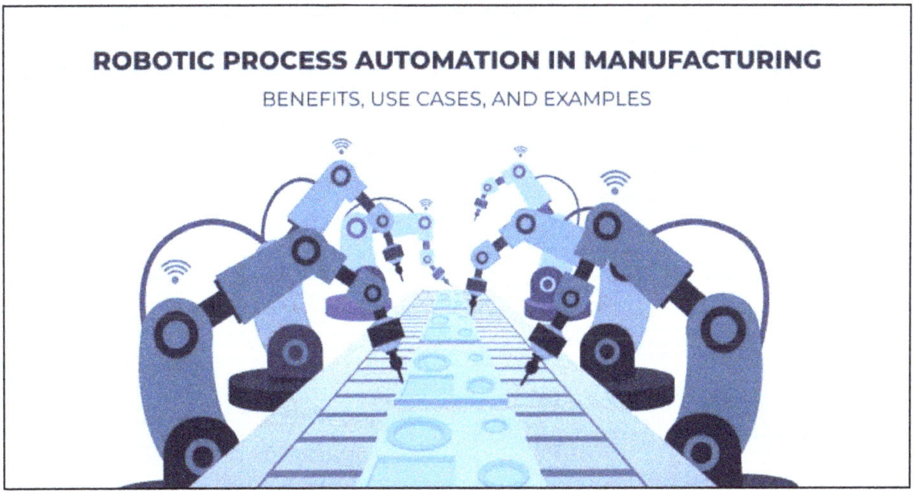

Figure 6.7 A representation of RPA in manufacturing [12].

6.4 Applications Of Robotic Process Automation In Manufacturing

RPA bots can automate a range of operations. Tasks related to inventory management and order processing, supply chain management, quality control, production monitoring, compliance and reporting, and invoice processing are most suitable for RPA-enabled automation. RPAs can be deployed in diverse forms to automate more complex processes across industries such as manufacturing, finance, and healthcare. HR, finance, and customer support departments also benefit from deploying RPA to automate manual processes. Common applications of RPA in manufacturing include the following [1,13-16]:

- *Manufacturing Automation:* This includes using advanced technology, including robotics, vision, and software, to streamline and optimize production processes. Manufacturing automation can take many forms, such as using autonomous robotics to handle parts and products in strategic areas. It can also include using artificial intelligence and high-speed cameras to find errors in products. Automation has become synonymous with using robotics and machines to reduce or replace work traditionally done by employees. But robotics is only one part of how automation works in the manufacturing industry. Controls engineers can program robotics to do the same task the same way every time, or, using more advanced technology, they can program them to be more flexible. Manufacturers who install robotics and automation solutions into their production lines can improve productivity, accuracy, repeatability, and quality. Figure 6.8 shows a typical example of manufacturing automation [17].

Figure 6.8 A typical example of manufacturing automation [17].

- *Administration:* This is one of the most fundamental examples of RPA being used to perform routine tasks. Manufacturing companies face plenty of issues when it comes to processing that can result in a considerable overload on the administration departments. This is where RPA serves as the magic wand for dealing with effectively managing administration. Manufacturing and administrative tasks are time-consuming. Employees can concentrate on other crucial tasks when these tasks are reduced in importance. The manufacturing industry has a lot of administrative tasks that get automated. Tasks that are simple to automate include attendance, action items, and meeting minutes.
- *Supply Chains:* Coordinating supply chain activities, such as procurement, logistics, and transportation, involves managing

multiple processes and stakeholders. Due to global geopolitical tensions, a supply chain may become a roller coaster for manufacturers. Supply chains have faced unprecedented disruptions in recent years, impacting manufacturers and logistics providers alike, along with their customers. Automation is transforming supply chains by enhancing efficiency, accuracy, and resilience in manufacturing operations. Within supply chain management, RPA can automate procurement, supplier management, inventory tracking, shipment tracking, supplier communications, and more, integrating with enterprise resource management (ERP) systems to reduce manual data entry. This speeds up invoice processing and purchase order approvals, and it optimizes logistics and freight scheduling.

- *Order Tracking*: Busy manufacturing teams can receive thousands of orders per month. RPA can help process and fulfil these orders by automating the entire process. Automating repetitive tasks in order tracking facilitates transparency in managing the flow of goods from the production line to the warehouse. RPA bots can track the status of shipments from suppliers in real time using tracking numbers, generate automated alerts for any delays or deviations from expected delivery times, and update internal inventory systems upon receipt of goods.

- *Data Management:* One of the biggest challenges in manufacturing is making sense of the vast amounts of data generated during production. Robotic process automation is great for the data management of an organization. RPA bots can collect, process, and analyze this data instantaneously. Data management involves the collection, validation, storage, protection, and processing of data to ensure its accessibility, reliability, and timeliness. RPA can automate data management tasks, such as data entry, data validation, and report generation. For example, an RPA bot can be programmed to automatically enter data into a system, validate it against predefined rules, and update the system with the validated data. The bot can generate reports based on the data, providing timely and accurate insights into various aspects of the manufacturing process. The bot can also validate the migrated data to ensure its accuracy and completeness.

- *Procurement Management:* Poor procurement data quality and a large number of operational tasks are the major challenges for procurement departments. RPA can help tackle these issues and contribute to the optimization of procurement operations within a manufacturing enterprise. After approving the vendor, procurement specialists can use RPA bots to generate contracts using prebuilt templates and vendor data, including the billing address and preferred payment period. RPA bots are also used to automatically set up new vendor accounts in the ERP.

- *Inventory Management:* The manufacturing industry has a lot of paperwork in inventory management. Inventory management is a fundamental part of manufacturing operations. Real-time monitoring of inventory levels is required to ensure that demand can be met. Inventory management is the activity of supervising and managing the movement of products into and out of a company's inventory. It is possible to automate inventory monitoring, stock-level notifications, and product reordering when the levels go below a set threshold. All this can be done with minimal human intervention. RPA in manufacturing provides inventory managers with real-time data about the inventory levels so that they can monitor these levels and make better decisions based on historical data. RPA can automate inventory management by automatically updating stock levels, generating purchase orders when necessary, and sending alerts when stock reaches a predefined threshold.

- *Waste Management:* One of the most important aspects of reducing production costs is waste management. Manufacturers keep seeking ways to cut down waste in production. Waste management can benefit manufacturing businesses from RPA. By digitizing numerous repetitive processes with RPA, manufacturers can identify quality issues with their products. RPA monitors the waste produced during production and adjusts the process accordingly. The RPA bots are great at fixing manufacturing hurdles like manual lapses, inventory wastage, and process wastage. The rule-based execution of RPA solutions brings down occurrences of errors and increases accuracy. Subsequently, wastage in all forms is reduced too.
- *Predictive Maintenance:* RPA can continuously collect real-time performance data from connected equipment and feed this information to AI algorithms. RPA and AI can automate quality assurance processes on assembly lines. Computer vision powered by AI can visually inspect products for defects. RPA bots can then perform automatic reworking or removal of defective items. This results in higher and more consistent product quality with less human effort.
- *Customer Service:* Customer experience is one of the crucial aspects of the success of any business. In the era of experience-as-a-economy, customer experience is one of the most important parts of the business. Unreliable customer service management with manual customer request handling

leads to errors in tracking information, and delayed response/resolution times leave customers unsatisfied. Resolving customer issues requires navigating through multiple business systems, which is time-consuming and requires a lot of effort. RPA can be a help in automating work in customer service, such as responding to common customer inquiries, updating customer records, and processing orders and returns. Your deployment can automatically respond to customer emails or chat messages that contain certain keywords, providing quick and consistent responses.

- *Bill of Materials (BOM):* The bill of materials is an important document that highlights what parts need to be manufactured. BOM is a central document in the manufacturing industry. It consists of a comprehensive record of materials as well as components that are required for creating a new item or product. The main aim of the document is to provide employees with all the data they require regarding their journey towards the advancement of new products, that is, information focusing on what, when, where, and how to buy. RPA, equipped with its ability to conduct quasi error-proof task functions, becomes a crucial requirement as it is programmed for precise and timely process completion. RPA technology allows for real-time management of the bill of materials. It ensures that everyone is on the same page and that any adjustments or changes are reflected in a single source of truth.

6.5 Benefits

RPA brings tangible benefits to companies across all industries, including manufacturing. The automation of mundane tasks enables companies to free up human workers to focus instead on innovation and problem-solving. In other words, manufacturers can reduce human intervention in repetitive tasks while using workers for more value-added responsibilities. This leads to increased productivity, significant cost savings, and enhanced decision-making through real-time data insights. Other benefits include the following [3,18]:

- *Cost Savings*: By saving hundreds of human workers' hours, RPA helps manufacturers decrease operational costs to free up financial resources for strategic initiatives. Wiping out costly errors and freeing up staff from mundane duties makes RPA an instrumental add-on to your cost-reduction strategy. Typical savings on current operational costs range from 25% to 80%, which can translate into tens of millions of dollars annually for some organizations. The speed and accuracy of automation help reduce administrative, prevention, appraisal, and internal/external failure costs.
- *Regulatory Compliance:* Manufacturers must adhere to several regulatory requirements. RPA can compile compliance data, generate reports, and even send them to regulators automatically, minimizing non-compliance risks. Apart from RPA-driven cost reduction, organizations also reap benefits like improved compliance, recognizing the impact of the technology on enhancing efficiency. With RPA's capability to cross-reference raw materials and testing results against regulatory requirements, update compliance documents in real time, and, overall, facilitate adherence to regulations, meeting even stringent standards. Governments around the world are enforcing stricter regulations on goods, with tight restrictions on various parts and practices.

- *Increased Productivity:* RPA transforms how dozens of routine but critical tasks are handled. The tireless digital workforce completes these tasks in seconds with near-zero error rates. Automation can be especially helpful when organizations experience a labor shortage. Any way you slice it, the outcome is freeing up thousands of labor hours yearly and increasing productivity as workers focus on higher-value, meaningful work.
- *Improved Quality:* Enhanced quality control is one of the most immediate benefits of RPA. High quality is always a matter of a strong reputation and profitability. Traditional bill of materials (BOM) management often suffers from manual errors. Incorrect quantities or assembly instructions, inconsistent updates, and difficulty tracking changes lead to defective products, wasted resources, and costly rework. Automation software accurately updates BOM data and transfers it into ERP systems, making sure nothing is overlooked, even when changes occur. In production lines, RPA maintains stringent quality specifications, reducing defects in final products. Bots consistently perform quality inspections, minimizing the risk of human oversight.

6.6 Challenges

While RPA brings numerous benefits, manufacturers should be aware of potential challenges. RPA software is static; it is not improved or changed based on the inputs or its results. Introducing RPA often requires a cultural shift within the organization. Employees may perceive automation as a threat to their jobs or may resist changes to established processes. One of the most common misconceptions about automation is that it will replace human workers. However, the reality is quite different. Other key challenges include the following [18]:

- *Complexity*: Manufacturing processes can be highly complex and interconnected, involving multiple systems, machines, and departments. Identifying and automating these processes requires a deep understanding of workflows and dependencies, which can pose challenges during implementation.
- *Limitations*: RPA handles repetitive, rule-based tasks within organizations. However, there are plenty of tasks that are less suitable for RPA, such as processing unstructured data or mimicking human decision-making. However, when augmented by AI, cognitive RPA can perform a blend of human and computer tasks, widening the scope of possible benefits within the manufacturing sector.
- *Legacy Systems*: Many manufacturing facilities still rely on legacy systems and equipment that may not be compatible with modern RPA technologies. Integrating RPA bots with existing IT infrastructure and ensuring seamless communication between different systems can be a technical challenge. RPA is adept at bridging the gap between legacy systems and modern infrastructure
- *Data Security:* Manufacturing operations generate vast amounts of sensitive data related to production, inventory, and customer information. Ensuring data security and compliance with regulatory requirements while handling and processing this data through RPA systems is crucial, but can be complex.
- *Skill Gap*: Implementing RPA requires skilled personnel who can design, develop, deploy, and maintain automation solutions. Finding individuals with expertise in RPA tools and

technologies, as well as providing ongoing training for employees, can be a challenge for manufacturing organizations. With the right investment, manufacturing management teams can ensure that delays caused by understaffing are a thing of the past while ensuring their productivity and efficiency grow as more processes are automated.

- *Scalability:* Over time, the manufacturing organization may look to scale its automation initiative, and the existing RPA solution may not be able to accommodate this growth. When choosing RPA technologies, manufacturing companies should evaluate the scalability of the potential platform.

6.7 Future Of Robotic Process Automation In Manufacturing

It is fascinating to consider how RPA could change the manufacturing sector in the future to deliver better products at lower costs. The ultimate goal for automation in manufacturing is not to automate a single task, but an entire process—and that requires multiple technologies, not just RPA. You need comprehensive, intelligent automation that uses a combination of RPA, AI, IoT, machine learning, and other technologies. The future of RPA in manufacturing promises deeper integration with these technologies, especially with artificial intelligence and IoT devices, automating complex workflows with minimal human intervention, minimizing errors, and further driving innovation and efficiency. Traditional RPA automates rule-based, repetitive tasks, but when combined with AI and

ML, it evolves into intelligent automation (IA). These technologies can be combined and used as key enablers for end-to-end process automation [19].

Automation and robotics solutions in manufacturing are expanding and will continue to change the manufacturing plant. The global manufacturing industry will face significant business obstacles in the coming years. International supply chain uncertainty, tax and transfer pricing reforms, a push for sustainability, a shortage of raw materials and components, and ageing IT infrastructures are among these. The future of labor in manufacturing is one where human ingenuity and robotic efficiency coexist. By embracing manufacturing automation, companies are not only addressing the immediate concerns of labor shortage and retention but are also investing in a future where their human workforce can engage in more strategic, creative, and technically demanding roles. As we look to the future, it is evident that the harmonious integration of human and machine labor is an achievable reality that promises to sustain the industry for generations to come [20].

6.8 Conclusion

Robotic process automation (RPA) is a technology that uses software robots to automate and streamline repetitive and rule-based tasks in various business processes. At its core, RPA involves creating a set of instructions that guide the software robots to perform specific tasks. The key advantage of RPA lies in its ability to perform tasks faster and more accurately than humans. In manufacturing, these tasks can range from data entry and reporting to routine inspections and quality control. Manufacturers are actively adopting RPA to automate voluminous and repetitive tasks that constitute their daily routines. RPA is reshaping manufacturing operations and driving unprecedented efficiency. RPA is here to stay.

In today's era of digital transformation, RPA is not just a competitive advantage; it is becoming a core pillar of modern manufacturing strategy. The next evolution of RPA is intelligent automation, which involves combining RPA with AI, machine learning, and predictive analytics. The future of manufacturing lies in the intelligent integration of these technologies. This allows bots not just to follow rules, but also to learn from data and make decisions. Add artificial intelligence (AI) and machine learning (ML) into the mix, and RPA can be taken to new heights.

Integrating robotic process automation is becoming a cornerstone in the modern manufacturing landscape, offering efficiencies that were previously unattainable.

This technology, once perceived as futuristic, has now become an essential tool for manufacturers aiming to stay competitive in an increasingly fast-paced market. The ability of RPA to automate certain repetitive, predictable, and rule-based processes traditionally handled by humans makes it a sought-after technology. It minimizes human errors and boosts business efficiency and productivity. It is becoming increasingly popular as a way for businesses to increase efficiency, cut expenses, and improve output.

More information about robotic process automation in manufacturing can be found in the books [21-26].

References

[1] A. Hand, "Unlocking efficiency: The role of robotic process automation in manufacturing," April 2025,

https://www.automate.org/industry-insights/benefits-rpa-manufacturing

[2] "How robotic process automation (RPA) is optimizing 'business-as-usual'" August 2021, https://medium.com/elucidate-ai/how-robotic-process-automation-rpa-is-optimizing-business-as-usual-1c5e5c46ef43

[3] "Manufacturing industry automation with RPA," https://www.keyence.com/products/software/rpa/industries/manufacturing.jsp

[4] M. N. O. Sadiku and J. O. Sadiku, "Robotic process automation in manufacturing," *International Journal of Trend in Scientific Research and Development*, vol. 10, no. 1, January-February, 2026, pp. 488-497.

[5] N. Komitsky, "Putting robotic process automation to work in the federal government,"

https://www.managementconcepts.com/resource/putting-robotic-process-automation-to-work-in-the-federal-government/

[6] "What is robotic process automation (RPA)? How does it work?" February 2023,

https://solidpro-es.com/what-is-robotic-process-automation-rpa-how-it-works/

[7] F. Caltin, "RPA in finance," February 2020,

https://www.plutushealthinc.com/post/rpa-in-finance

[8] "Absolutely everything you need to know about robotic process automation,"

https://www.blueprism.com/guides/robotic-process-automation-rpa/

[9] S. Donnelly, "5 Benefits of robotic process automation in finance," September 2022,

https://www.financealliance.io/5-benefits-of-robotic-process-automation-in-finance/

[10] "Robotic process automation in finance," September 2023,

https://kmbs.konicaminolta.us/blog/robotic-process-automation-in-finance/

[11] "Robotic process automation in finance,"

https://planergy.com/blog/robotic-process-automation-finance/

[12] P. Peranzo, "Robotic process automation in manufacturing: Benefits, use cases, and examples," October 2023,

https://imaginovation.net/blog/rpa-in-manufacturing/

[13] A. Astakhov, “RPA in manufacturing: Game-changing benefits and use cases with the fastest ROI,” June 2024, https://www.instinctools.com/blog/rpa-in-manufacturing-industry/

[14] S. Parikh, “The role of automation in the manufacturing industry,” September 2023,

https://nividous.com/blogs/rpa-in-manufacturing-industry

[15] “Get to market faster with RPA for manufacturing,”

https://www.1rivet.com/insights/rpa-in-manufacturing

[16] A. Mishra, “RPA in manufacturing: Automated industrial to streamline manufacturing & boost productivity,” June 2023,

https://outworkssolutions.com/technology-blogs/software-consulting/robotic-process-automation/rpa-in-manufacturing-automated-industrial-to-streamline-manufacturing-and-boost-productivity/

[17] “Benefits of manufacturing process automation,” June 2020,

https://illinoispulleyandgear.com/blogs/blog/benefits-of-robotic-process-automation

[18] https://rpa.synapseindia.com/blog/rpa-benefits-challenges-and-use-case-in-manufacturing/

[19] “Robotic process automation in manufacturing industry,” May 2025,

https://erpsoftwareblog.com/2025/05/robotic-process-automation-in-manufacturing-industry/

[20] "The future of labor in manufacturing: Manufacturing process automation,"

https://onexia.com/blog/the-future-of-labor-in-manufacturing-manufacturing-process-automation/

[21] Jacob, *Achieving Excellence in Manufacturing Through Robotic Process Automation: An Engineer's Perspective.* Sunshine, 2023.

[22] H. Mahey, *Robotic Process Automation with Automation Anywhere: Techniques to Fuel Business Productivity And Intelligent Automation Using RPA.* Packt Publishing, 2020.

[23] T. Taulli, *The Robotic Process Automation Handbook: A Guide to Implementing RPA Systems.* Apress, 2020.

[24] R. Fantina, A. Storozhuk, and K. Goyal, *Introducing Robotic Process Automation to Your Organization: A Guide for Business Leaders*. Apress, 2021.

[25] C. Czarnecki and P. Fettke (eds.), *Robotic Process Automation: Management, Technology, Applications.* De Gruyter, 2021.

[26] C. Juarez, *Unleashing Efficiency: The Power of Robotic Process Automation (RPA).* Independently Published, 2023.

CHAPTER 7
ROBOTIC PROCESS AUTOMATION IN TELECOMMUNICATIONS

"Everything comes from everything, and everything is made out of everything, and everything returns into everything."
Leonardo Da Vinci.

7.1 Introduction

Automation is the only way to stay competitive. Before automation, the team spent hours chasing overdue invoices. By implementing robotic process automation (RPA), telecom companies can significantly reduce the time and effort required to perform repetitive tasks, allowing human resources to focus on more strategic activities. With RPA, payment status is verified automatically, reminders are sent on time, and subscription actions happen instantly. The result is fewer overdue invoices, faster resolution, and significant time savings for the operations team. Payments, device logistics, service fulfillment, and order confirmations are orchestrated through RPA, transforming complex integrations into one seamless, end-to-end process.

The telecommunications industry is constantly evolving, driven by the need to manage massive data volumes, enhance customer experience, and streamline operations. Telecom companies have been among the most active adopters of RPA, and with reason. The quantity of documents they process and interactions with customers, partners, and contractors dictate the need for intelligent automation at multiple levels. Integrating RPA can help telecom companies simplify the handling of operational tasks and generate lasting revenue streams. Figure 7.1 provides a definition of robotic process automation [1], while Figure 7.2 shows the complexity of a telecommunications network [2].

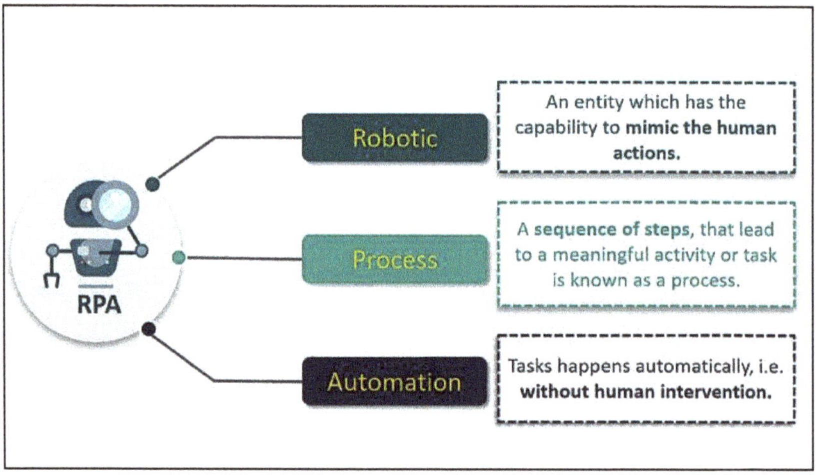

Figure 7.1 A definition of robotic process automation [1].

Figure 7.2 Complexity of telecommunications network [2].

Robotic process automation (RPA) involves the use of software robots to automate routine tasks that were traditionally performed by human workers. In the telecom sector, these tasks often include data entry, invoicing, order processing, and customer service operations. RPA in telecom has emerged as a game-changing solution, enabling telecom companies to automate repetitive tasks, reduce operational costs, and improve service efficiency. At the most basic level, RPA automates simple data entry tasks that the telecom industry abounds in. RPA allows telecom companies to focus more on innovation and less on manual labor. This automation leads to improved efficiency, lower operational costs, streamlined billing processes, accurate billing, and enhanced customer satisfaction [3].

This chapter examines the role of RPA in telecommunications. It begins with explaining the concept of robotic process automation (RPA). It describes RPA in telecommunications and provides some of its applications. It highlights the benefits and challenges of RPA in telecommunications. It predicts the future of RPA in telecommunications. The last section concludes with comments.

7.2 What Is Robotic Process Automation?

Among the various forms of artificial intelligence, RPA stands out for its potential to significantly increase workforce productivity by reducing or eliminating the need to do repetitive tasks manually. Popular applications of RPA include data entry, data reconciliation, spreadsheet manipulation, systems integration, automated data reporting, analytics, email notifications, acquisitions, administrative services, finance, human resources, mission assurance, strategic communications, travel reimbursements, claims processing, and customer outreach and communications. These are just a few examples of the ways RPA is being used to remove the burden of manual, repetitive, and duplicative tasks from public service workers [4].

Robotic process automation is a form of automation software. It is a technology that can automate repetitive, rules-based tasks. Like an Excel macro operating within a spreadsheet, RPA can record actions performed across a personal computer, access systems, and perform specific tasks for human users. It uses software robots, more commonly called "bots," that mimic basic human-computer interactions. Figure 7.3 shows the symbol of RPA [5], while Figure 7.4 shows processes that RPA can automate [6]. Most industries use RPA. The government does too. Due to the repetitive nature of some tasks, the probability of human error increases. One way to eliminate errors is by using RPA.

Figure 7.3 Symbol of RPA [5].

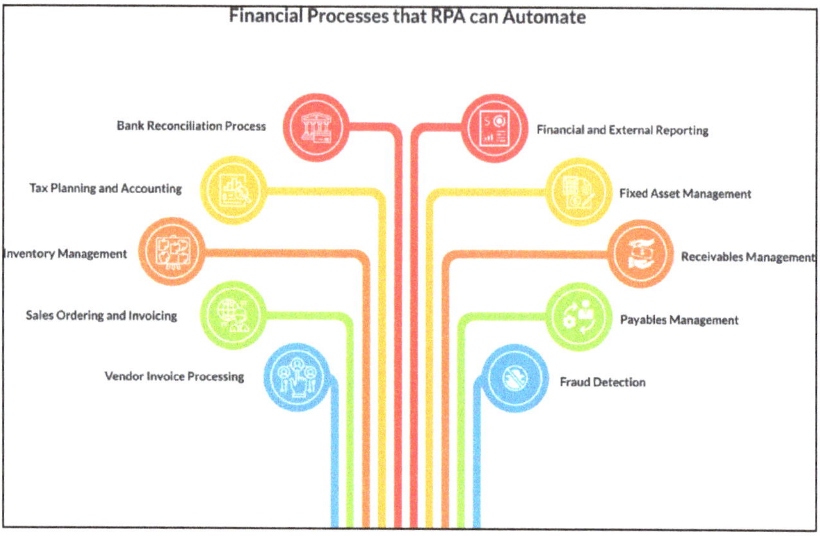

Figure 7.4 Processes that RPA can automate [6].

Robotic process automation solutions fall into three key categories: attended RPA, unattended RPA, and hybrid RPA, as shown in Figure 7.5 [7].

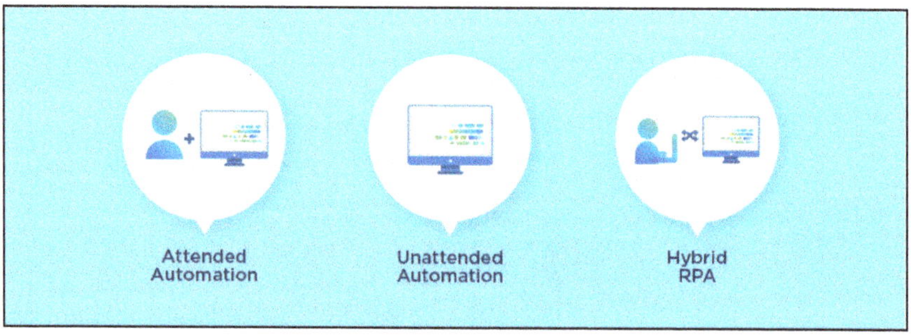

Figure 7.5 Three key categories of RPA [7].

Robotic process automation is a type of software that mimics the activity of a human being in carrying out a task within a process. It is a technology that automates repetitive tasks using software robots. RPA uses a set of automation tools to automate repetitive tasks and manual processes performed electronically. Since RPA can automate tasks that are rule-based, manual, repetitive, and tedious, delivering the highest levels of accuracy and eradicating human errors, it is a seamless fit for the finance industry. Here are some specific examples of what RPA in finance can do [8]:

- Opening emails and joining attachments
- Automatically logging into various applications on the web
- Shifting folders and files
- Copying and pasting
- Completing forms
- Collecting data from databases and the web
- Making calculations
- Connecting to system API
- Extracting structured data from documents
- Gathering stats from social media
- Following if/then decisions and rules

Some of these tasks are displayed in Figure 7.6 [7].

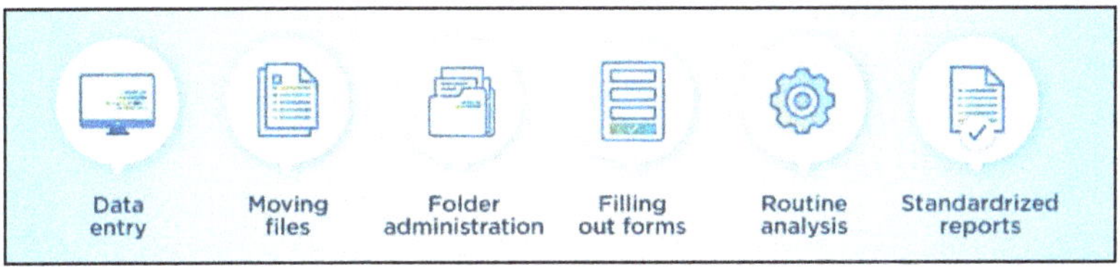

Figure 7.6 Some tasks RPA can perform [7].

At its core, robotic process automation (RPA) is a tool designed to mimic rule-based business processes, performing them seamlessly and without fatigue. RPA is a rule-driven method that is limited in its application. The technology functions much like a Microsoft Excel macro; the key difference is in power and reach. It follows set rules, similar to how an Excel macro works, to do things like move files or log into accounts. Growing as a popular solution in finance and accounting, RPA refers to software technology or "software robots" with artificial intelligence (AI) and machine learning (ML) capabilities. The "software robots" have the ability to learn and complete a high volume of rules-based, repetitive tasks and business processes. They have the capacity to operate much faster than humans, with 100% precision and reliability, working around the clock.

Finance and human resources are just two examples of departments likely to have many use cases that RPA can help solve. Some examples of good use cases for RPA in finance include processing customer orders, ensuring timely vendor payments, and managing period-end financial close processes. For human resources, some examples include employee onboarding, time tracking, and leave of absence management. Processes where human judgment is needed are not appropriate for RPA since RPA automations rely on clear, consistently applied rules [9].

Along with RPA, one should be aware of both business process automation (BPA) and digital process automation (DPA) – two commonly used automation technologies that robotics process automation can be paired with to optimize and streamline a digital transformation. BPA refers to the use of technology to automate complex, multi-step workflows, typically very specific to a company's core business functions. DPA offers dual power by automating processes from end to end and optimizing common workflows that involve external human interactions (i.e., sales, management). Separately, RPA and AI are quite powerful, but leveraging them together is undoubtedly advantageous to any financial institution. When deployed together, AI is the "brains" behind RPA's bots [10].

7.3 Robotic Process Automation In Telecommunications

Today's communication service providers (CSPs) operate in an increasingly competitive environment. Driven by the Internet of Things (IoT), 5G, and edge computing, the utilization of telecom services is exploding. This surging demand presents significant revenue opportunities for CSPs, but it also poses substantial challenges. Telecom companies have found that even basic organizational functions like customer support and order fulfillment are growing increasingly complicated. Many face heightened regulations, skills shortages, and rising customer expectations. To meet these challenges, telecom service providers are turning to automation. Robotic process automation (RPA) is a method of automation that uses software robots to carry out simple, structured, and repetitive business processes. RPA can reduce costs, increase quality, deliver greater value, and provide a better experience for customers—all while freeing up employees to do more high-value, meaningful work [11]. Figure 7.7 shows a representation of RPA in telecommunication [12].

Figure 7.7 A representation of RPA in telecommunication [12].

7.4 Applications Of Robotic Process Automation In Telecommunications

Telecom use cases for robotic process automation are extremely diverse and depend primarily on an organization's existing business processes and the pain points and bottlenecks the organization is striving to eliminate. They cover quite a lot of services, such as on-time billing, payment processing, customer service, number portability, speeding up the document verification and SIM allotment process, data entry, data processing, data management, and much more. Common applications of RPA in the telecom industry include the following [2,13,14]:

- *Customer Support*: One of the areas where RPA truly shines is customer support. Dealing with a massive number of queries and converting them into categorized support tickets according to their content and service-level agreement (SLA) rules is a labor-intensive task. RPA bots do a great job analyzing and interpreting incoming email and chat requests, responding to some immediately with predefined answers from the company's knowledge base while categorizing others and assigning them to a particular support group.
- *Invoice Processing*: Managing accounts receivable and payable for millions of subscribers and hundreds of vendors is challenging, especially considering the ramifications of invoice errors. Well-implemented business support systems (BSS) automation with strategically embedded RPA bots helps automate this complex and tedious workflow, making it less prone to errors, delays, and data duplication. From invoice discounts for early payments and higher vendor loyalty to access to better offers and improved employee satisfaction — all of these perks come as a result of letting RPA bots take care of time-sensitive and repetitive financial operations that employers would otherwise get swamped with.
- *Network Monitoring*: Telecom networks are vast and complex, requiring constant monitoring to ensure they operate smoothly. Traditional network management involves manual processes that are time-consuming and prone to errors. RPA in telecom automates network monitoring, allowing telecom companies to detect and resolve issues more quickly. RPA bots can monitor network performance in real-time, identify potential issues, and trigger automated responses to resolve them.

- *Network Maintenance:* Network issues can often be resolved (and even prevented) without replacing hardware or performing complex software reconfigurations. In many cases, preemptively increasing the threshold of a particular value or restarting a service/hardware unit is enough to bring your network status back into the green zone. RPA in telecommunications companies can be effectively combined with AI to create highly autonomous intelligent bots that monitor network performance and replace live personnel in cases where human intervention is not required.
- *Network Management:* As the level of traffic and complications in the distributed networks increases, telecom network management is becoming difficult for service providers because it involves navigating complex applications, manually retrieving data, and large amounts of customer-related information retrieval to enhance the efficacy of the network infrastructure. Deployment of RPA technology enables telecom providers to make use of automated solutions for monotonous tasks such as event and diagnostic management, thus allowing network engineers to give more attention to complex processes.
- *Data Management:* Telecom providers generate billions of data bytes every day, especially the larger players in the business. Storing this data, easing out the unnecessary bits, and translating the required ones into business-ready information could be a daunting and time-consuming task. As the telecom industry depends on huge sets of data stored in various file formats, RPA can be utilized to bring significant changes. RPA bots can automate data management tasks, such as data entry, validation, and reporting, ensuring that data is accurate, up-to-date, and readily available for decision-making. In order to support rapid growth, telecom companies

need to solve the problems posed by large volumes of operational processes managing data, controlling costs, increasing business agility, acquiring talent, and developing new services.

- *Data Entry:* Data entry jobs have always been associated with high intensity, tediousness, and a significant risk of employee burnout — all of which lead to errors and data corruption. This is one of the best telecommunication use cases for RPA, as bots are a perfect solution for high-volume, ultra-fast, concurrent data entry through standard forms. Besides obvious advantages like the speed of document processing, fewer data entry errors, and higher customer satisfaction, setting up an effective RPA workflow can free up valuable human resources so people can attend to tasks that generate more added value for the company.
- *Debt Collection:* RPA helps telecom companies identify and collect what their organization is owed on the respective due dates. The role of automation in the telecom industry can help the organization determine and collect what its telecom companies owe on the due dates. A robust RPA platform can automate various steps of the debt collection process, such as payment information updates, due dates, payment reconciliation, and urgent escalations. This helps the employees to be more productive by worrying less about the collection and being more concerned about the distribution of their services.
- *Fraud Detection:* The telecom industry is highly susceptible to fraud, which can result in significant financial losses. Traditional fraud detection methods are often reactive and can be slow to identify suspicious activities. RPA in telecom enhances fraud detection by automating the monitoring

and analysis of transactions in real-time. RPA can analyze large volumes of data to detect patterns indicative of fraudulent activities. It can quickly flag suspicious transactions or activities for further investigation, thus helping telecom companies mitigate risks.

7.5 Benefits

RPA is becoming a standard way of doing business. It simplifies operations, reduces costs, improves accuracy, and strengthens customer service. One of the key advantages of RPA is its ability to streamline core business processes. Bots are also much less likely to make errors when moving data between systems. Automation makes it easier to monitor network performance, plan for infrastructure expansion, and optimize as necessary. That means telecom companies spend less time and money on maintenance and more time reaping the rewards of an efficient network. Other benefits of RPA in telecommunications include the following [12,15]:

- *Cost Reduction*: One of the most significant benefits of telecom automation is cost reduction. By automating routine tasks, companies can significantly reduce operational costs. This allows them to allocate resources more effectively and invest in other areas of growth.
- *Accuracy and Speed:* Telecom companies deal with vast amounts of data daily, from customer information to billing details. Manually handling this data can lead to errors and inefficiencies. RPA can automate data entry and validation, ensuring accuracy and speed. Automation eliminates the risk

of human error in data processing and other repetitive tasks, leading to more reliable outcomes and better decision-making.

- *Customer Satisfaction:* As telecom technology has advanced, so have the public's expectations. Customers want a speedy resolution to their requests, but they do not want customer service to feel mechanical. Customer satisfaction drops by 30% if it takes more than a day to resolve an issue with a telecom provider. Automating customer service processes leads to faster response times and improved service quality, strengthening customer relationships. Individual consumers and enterprise customers all rely on high-speed, high-powered communication and computing capabilities to process the growing amounts of data they use daily. RPA can play a key role in attracting and retaining more customers by creating more compelling and personalized customer experiences. RPA can also speed up the process of provisioning services to users while enabling customer service reps to deliver a more personal touch.
- *Employee Empowerment*: By letting robots handle repetitive tasks, employees can focus on more interesting work, which boosts job satisfaction and helps them grow professionally. While robots make things run smoother, it is the human touch (our ability to think outside the box) that really makes a company shine. However, your people and human creativity are still your strongest assets.
- *Scalability*: RPA bots have nearly infinite scalability. RPA can be seen as a scalable workforce that never rests or loses focus, and performs its tasks with predictable efficiency. RPA solutions can be scaled up or down based on business needs, providing the flexibility required to adapt to market changes and customer demands. Telecom automation with RPA allows

companies to scale their operations more easily. If a communications service provider (CSP) chooses an RPA solution with concurrent execution built in, teams can run multiple bots at once on a single machine. This allows for multiple data transfers between multiple systems simultaneously, greatly accelerating the speed of automated processes.

7.6 Challenges

Like any new technology, RPA has its challenges. The telecom industry faces several challenges, including managing vast amounts of data, ensuring regulatory compliance, and maintaining complex networks. Telecom providers have to be ready to cope with increased service demands whenever the need arises. With increasing competition in the telecom space, newer and more unique challenges emerge in providing innovative services to customers. Other challenges include the following [16]:

- *High Cost*: Managing and developing RPA involves significant financial investments, which is a major concern. The initial setup requires considerable expenses for specialized software, hardware, and skilled personnel. Additionally, ongoing maintenance adds to the financial burden as organizations strive to keep automated processes running smoothly. Investing in RPA development and management demands a substantial financial commitment both initially and continuously.
- *Data Security*: A major concern is data security. Bots often deal with sensitive customer information, so strict policies and

monitoring are needed. Consumers are increasingly aware of data security, influencing telecom providers to implement secure RPA solutions that protect user information.

- *Transparency:* Consumers desire transparency in service processes; RPA helps telecom companies provide clear, consistent communication and updates.
- *Legacy Systems:* There is a lack of a safe application testing environment due to legacy systems, along with the presence of older operating systems, necessitating additional care and effort to ensure smooth application rollouts. Use APIs or middleware to ensure that RPA solutions integrate effectively with older systems.
- *Regulatory Compliance*: Telecom companies operate in a highly regulated environment, with strict requirements for data security, customer privacy, and reporting. The Federal Communications Commission (FCC) subjects the telecom industry to heavy regulation, including antitrust, licensing, and pricing laws. Staying compliant with regulatory mandates can be time-consuming and labor-intensive, but RPA can make it less of an administrative burden. All a company has to do is schedule a group of unattended bots to regularly collect relevant compliance data from specified systems and compile it all in a central spreadsheet. RPA bots can automatically generate compliance reports, validate data against regulatory requirements, and ensure that all necessary documentation is in place.

7.7 Future Of Robotic Process Automation In Telecommunications

The telecommunications industry is witnessing a significant shift towards automation, with robotic process automation (RPA) becoming a critical component of operational strategies. The integration of RPA into telecom operations is just the beginning of a broader shift towards automation. As we look ahead, the telecom industry is ready for changes driven by advancements in RPA and automation technologies. RPA technologies are expected to become even more sophisticated, integrating seamlessly with AI and machine learning to deliver enhanced capabilities. RPA, combined with AI processing, can help automate network optimization so that faults are addressed in real-time with minimal human intervention.

The RPA in the telecommunications market is expected to witness sustained global growth driven by innovation, digitization, and emerging economy participation. Telecom companies will likely experience a paradigm shift as automation takes over more of the traditional roles performed by human workers. This shift will free up human capital for strategic and creative tasks, fostering innovation and improving customer relationships. With automation handling the bulk of routine operations, telecom companies will be able to offer more personalized and responsive services, enhancing customer satisfaction. As the telecom industry continues to evolve, embracing technologies like RPA will be essential for staying competitive and driving efficiency [17].

7.8 Conclusion

The telecom industry, known for its complexity and large-scale operations, is undergoing a significant transformation with the adoption of robotic process automation (RPA). RPA can be a real game-changer for your telecom business. From optimizing customer support to ensuring accurate invoice processing, RPA is a tool to boost your business operations. RPA in telecom is considered one of the primary means of maintaining a consistently high level of business support systems efficiency. By implementing RPA in telecom, companies can streamline their operations, improve accuracy, and free up employees to focus on more strategic tasks.

Companies that invest in upgrading their telecom infrastructure and embrace cutting-edge automation technologies will gain a competitive advantage. These companies will be able to deliver services more efficiently and at a lower cost, while also adapting swiftly to market demands. To maintain competitiveness in this rapidly evolving landscape, businesses must stay abreast of technological trends and be willing to invest in RPA and related innovations. By adopting these technologies, telecom companies can gain deeper insights into customer behavior, optimize network performance, and create new revenue streams. More information about robotic process automation in the telecommunications industry can be found in the books [18,19].

References

[1] "How robotic process automation (RPA) is optimizing 'business-as-usual'" August 2021, https://medium.com/elucidate-ai/how-robotic-process-automation-rpa-is-optimizing-business-as-usual-1c5e5c46ef43

[2] "Process automation solutions for the telecom industry,"

https://flobotics.io/telecom/

[3] M. N. O. Sadiku and J. O. Sadiku, "Robotic process automation in telecommunications," *International Journal of Trend in Scientific Research and Development,* vol. 10, no. 1, January-February 2026, pp. 508-516.

[4] N. Komitsky, "Putting robotic process automation to work in the federal government,"

https://www.managementconcepts.com/resource/putting-robotic-process-automation-to-work-in-the-federal-government/

[5] "What is robotic process automation (RPA)? How does it work?" February 2023,

https://solidpro-es.com/what-is-robotic-process-automation-rpa-how-it-works/

[6] F. Caltin, "RPA in finance," February 2020,

https://www.plutushealthinc.com/post/rpa-in-finance

[7] "Absolutely everything you need to know about robotic process automation,"

https://www.blueprism.com/guides/robotic-process-automation-rpa/

[8] S. Donnelly, "5 Benefits of robotic process automation in finance," September 2022,

https://www.financealliance.io/5-benefits-of-robotic-process-automation-in-finance/

[9] "Robotic process automation in finance," September 2023,

https://kmbs.konicaminolta.us/blog/robotic-process-automation-in-finance/

[10] "Robotic process automation in finance,"

https://planergy.com/blog/robotic-process-automation-finance/

[11] "Robotic process automation for carriers,"

https://www.uipath.com/resources/automation-whitepapers/robotic-process-automation-in-telecommunications-csps

[12] A. Nallasivam, "RPA use cases in the telecommunication industry,"

https://www.claysys.com/blog/rpa-in-telecommunication-industry/

[13] R. Makarchuk, "RPA in telecom industry: Use cases & business benefits," February 2024,

https://intellias.com/future-of-rpa-in-telecom/

[14] R. Rajeev, “Thirteen use cases of robotic process automation (RPA) in telecom,” September 2023,

https://www.managedoutsource.com/blog/thirteen-use-cases-robotic-process-automation-rpa-telecom/

[15] “8 Ways RPA is helping transform the telecom industry,”

https://www.ibm.com/think/topics/rpa-for-telecom

[16] “Leading telecom transforms customer experience with nice robotic process automation,”

http://crystalcomm.ge/?p=846

[17] J. Pencek, “Expected changes in 2025: A glimpse into the future of telecom,”

https://www.vatic-outsourcing.com/2025-rpa-revolutionizing-telecom

[18] H. Mahey, *Robotic Process Automation with Automation Anywhere: Techniques to Fuel Business Productivity And Intelligent Automation Using RPA.* Packt Publishing, 2020.

[19] C. Czarnecki and P. Fettke (eds.), *Robotic Process Automation: Management, Technology, Applications.* De Gruyter, 2021.

CHAPTER 8
ROBOTIC PROCESS AUTOMATION IN SUPPLY CHAIN

"Try not to become a man of success. *Rather, become a man of value."*
Albert Einstein.

8.1 Introduction

Supply chains are networks of companies, resources, and people involved in producing and delivering products. They serve as an essential link between manufacturers and consumers. Vital components of supply chains include retailers, vendors, producers, warehouses, transportation or logistics companies, and distribution centers. Unfortunately, many supply chain tasks are incredibly time-consuming and error-sensitive when done manually, leading to inefficiencies and costly delays. This is where RPA emerges as a game-changer and solves these problems. RPA can take repetitive tasks off your plate so your organization can concentrate on important, human-centric tasks. Unlike traditional automation that requires deep programming, RPA operates at the user interface level, making it easier to deploy and manage. RPA automates routine tasks, ensuring faster, more accurate, and more efficient operations across the supply chain. RPA leverages software robots to perform tasks such as processing orders, updating inventory records, and managing shipments, thereby allowing supply chain teams to focus on more strategic initiatives. Figure 8.1 defines robotic process automation [1], while Figure 8.2 shows a supply chain team [2].

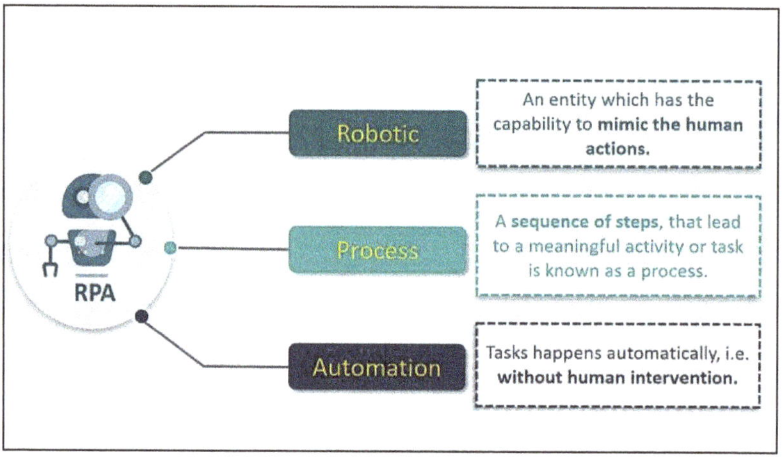

Figure 8.1 A definition of robotic process automation [1].

Figure 8.2 Supply chain team [2].

All departments across the organization can benefit from implementing automation solutions. One technical method for automating corporate activities is robotic process automation (RPA). RPA is a technology that uses software robots, or "bots," to automate repetitive and rule-based tasks usually performed by humans. These bots mimic human actions like reading emails, processing invoices, entering data, or tracking shipments, but they do it faster, with greater accuracy, and 24/7. RPA is a part of digital transformation since it enables businesses to automate procedures, increase accuracy, and free up human resources for strategic work. Supply chain automation uses RPA to make supply chain processes lean and efficient. Supply chain automation tools give companies new ways to cope with uncertainty and keep business processes and products moving. Robotics in the supply chain will decrease manual labor, freeing up staff members to concentrate on more crucial tasks and lowering data analysis errors [3].

In this chapter, we explore the profound effects of RPA on supply chain logistics. The chapter begins with explaining the concept of robotic process automation (RPA). It describes RPA in the supply chain and provides some of its applications. It highlights the benefits and challenges of RPA in the supply chain. It predicts the future of RPA in the supply chain. The last section concludes with comments.

8.2 What Is Robotic Process Automation?

Among the various forms of artificial intelligence, RPA stands out for its potential to significantly increase workforce productivity by reducing or eliminating the need to do repetitive tasks manually. Popular applications of RPA include data entry, data reconciliation, spreadsheet manipulation, systems integration, automated data reporting, analytics, email notifications, acquisitions, administrative services, finance, human resources, mission assurance, strategic communications, travel reimbursements, claims processing, and customer outreach and communications. These are just a few examples of the ways RPA is being used to remove the burden of manual, repetitive, and duplicative tasks from public service workers [4].

Robotic process automation is a form of automation software. It is a technology that can automate repetitive, rules-based tasks. Like an Excel macro operating within a spreadsheet, RPA can record actions performed across a personal computer, access systems, and perform specific tasks for human users. It uses software robots, more commonly called "bots," that mimic basic human-computer interactions. Figure 8.3 shows the symbol of RPA [5], while Figure 8.4 shows processes that RPA can automate [6]. Most industries use RPA. The government does too. Due to the repetitive nature of some tasks, the probability of human error increases. One way to eliminate errors is by using RPA. Robotic process automation solutions fall into three key categories: attended RPA, unattended RPA, and hybrid RPA, as shown in Figure 8.5 [7].

Figure 8.3 Symbol of RPA [5].

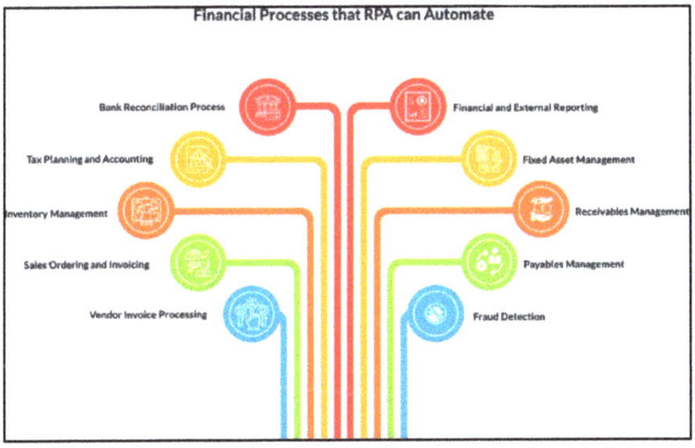

Figure 8.4 Processes that RPA can automate [6].

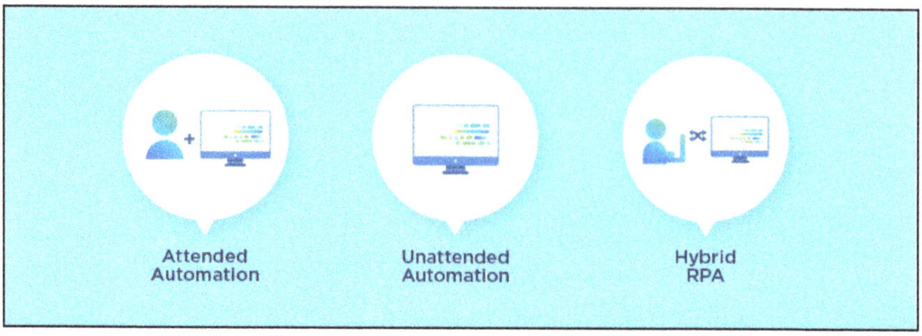

Figure 8.5 Three key categories of RPA [7].

Robotic process automation is a type of software that mimics the activity of a human being in carrying out a task within a process. It is a technology that automates repetitive tasks using software robots. RPA uses a set of automation tools to automate repetitive tasks and manual processes performed electronically. Since RPA can automate tasks that are rule-based, manual, repetitive, and tedious, delivering the highest levels of accuracy and eradicating human errors, it is a seamless fit for the finance industry. Here are some specific examples of what RPA in finance can do [8]:

- Opening emails and joining attachments
- Automatically logging into various applications on the web
- Shifting folders and files
- Copying and pasting
- Completing forms
- Collecting data from databases and the web
- Making calculations

- Connecting to system API
- Extracting structured data from documents
- Gathering stats from social media
- Following if/then decisions and rules

Some of these tasks are displayed in Figure 8.6 [7].

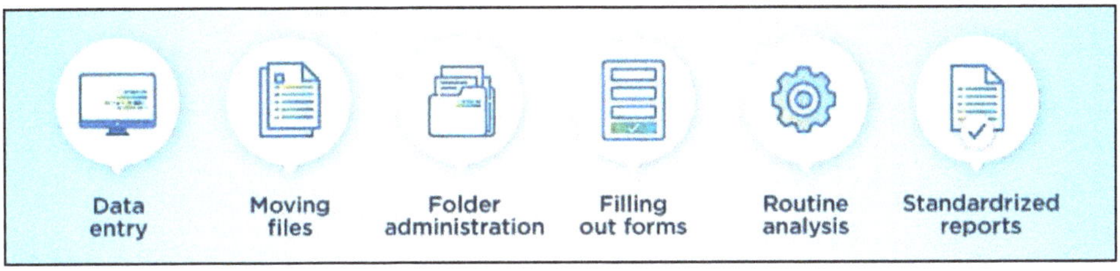

Figure 8.6 Some tasks RPA can perform [7].

At its core, robotic process automation (RPA) is a tool designed to mimic rule-based business processes, performing them seamlessly and without fatigue. RPA is a rule-driven method that is limited in its application. The technology functions much like a Microsoft Excel macro; the key difference is in power and reach. It follows set rules, similar to how an Excel macro works, to do things like move files or log into accounts. Growing as a popular solution in finance and accounting, RPA refers to software technology or "software robots" with artificial intelligence (AI) and machine learning (ML) capabilities. The "software robots" have the ability to learn and complete a high volume of rules-based, repetitive tasks and business processes. They have the capacity to operate much faster than humans, with 100% precision and reliability, working around the clock.

Finance and human resources are just two examples of departments likely to have many use cases that RPA can help solve. Some examples of good use cases for RPA in finance include processing customer orders, ensuring timely vendor payments, and managing period-end financial close processes. For human resources, some examples include employee onboarding, time tracking, and leave of absence management. Processes where human judgment is needed are not appropriate for RPA since RPA automations rely on clear, consistently applied rules [9].

Along with RPA, one should be aware of both business process automation (BPA) and digital process automation (DPA) – two commonly used automation technologies that robotics process automation can be paired with to optimize and streamline a digital transformation. BPA refers to the use of technology to automate complex, multi-step workflows, typically very specific to a company's core business functions. DPA offers dual power by automating processes from end to end and optimizing common workflows that involve external human interactions (i.e., sales, management). Separately, RPA and AI are quite powerful, but leveraging them together is undoubtedly advantageous to any financial institution. When deployed together, AI is the "brains" behind RPA's bots [10].

8.3 Robotic Process Automation In Supply Chain

The supply chain and logistics department is a cornerstone of modern business operations, responsible for managing everything from procurement and inventory management to order fulfillment and shipment tracking. Traditional methods of handling procurement, inventory, and order fulfillment are often slow, error-prone, and costly. In their pursuit of efficiency and smooth workflows, industries are turning to robotic process automation (RPA) as a game-changing element in supply chain logistics. RPA is a software technology that harnesses artificial intelligence and machine learning to simplify monotonous and manual tasks such as entering data, generating reports, and managing inventory. RPA, which uses smart bots to handle monotonous tasks, is altering how organizations handle their supply chains. This technology is taking over routine activities like data entry, tracking orders, and processing invoices. Businesses that implement RPA can automate various aspects of their supply chain operations. This results in increased efficiency and a reduced need for human intervention [11].

Robotic process automation in supply chain refers to the application of software tools to automate repetitive, rule-based tasks across various stages of supply chain management. RPA is revolutionizing supply chain management by automating mundane and repetitive tasks, allowing businesses to operate faster and with greater accuracy. When applied to supply chain management, RPA offers game-changing potential. From procurement to delivery, bots can streamline operations and improve decision-making. There are many RPA solutions on the market, and not all of them are good for your specific needs. A good starting point for an RPA solution is to look for one that provides you with full scalability and integration capabilities.

8.4 Applications Of Robotic Process Automation In Supply Chain

The transformative power of RPA is evident in real-world applications across industries, including supply chain management. RPA has numerous applications across the supply chain. Some of the most popular applications include the following [12,13]:

- *Order Management:* Order management is the heartbeat of any supply chain. It is a crucial part of the supply chain and is where much of the complexity in supply networks comes in. Here, order management refers to everything related to tracking, capturing, fulfilling, and managing customer orders. It contains many repetitive steps, making it a prime candidate for supply chain automation. RPA can handle complex workflows. With RPA in play, handling orders becomes a breeze. Incorporating RPA into the system automates the entire order processing journey – from double-checking customer details to promptly updating inventory levels and swiftly generating shipping labels. RPA can save time by verifying orders, pulling data from multiple systems, and eliminating duplicate orders, all without human input. Smart bots can work 24/7, ensuring that orders are managed effectively even when workers are not in the office. Order processing automation helps us save time by using bots to handle data entry, track orders, and update customer records. These tools connect with warehouse management systems to check stock levels fast.

- *Warehousing:* No matter what product a company sells or in which industry a company belongs, you need warehouses to store products at strategic locations. Managing a large number of products is not an easy job in warehouses. In warehouses, automation has turned what was once the slow, manual process of locating products into a veritable snap, with finely tuned robots gliding across the floor, fetching items from shelves, and delivering them directly to packing stations. Instead of workers literally having to walk miles each day retrieving products, robots handle this busy work in a fraction of the time. This both speeds up order fulfillment and maximizes the use of both warehouse space and personnel. Figure 8.7 shows a robot used in managing stock in a warehouse [2].

Figure 8.7 A robot used in managing stock in a warehouse [2].

- *Invoice Management:* Manual invoice handling can be slow and error-prone. Companies that rely on manual invoice creation often encounter delays, errors, and discrepancies. Invoice management is one of the top use cases for RPA across sectors, and with good reason. Invoicing and payments involve a lot of necessary but tedious steps. Invoicing robots can download invoices, scan or read paper invoices using OCR, capture data from emails, validate invoices, monitor payment deadlines, and streamline invoice acceptance. RPA handles invoice processing much faster than humans. It checks data on invoices, matches them with orders and receipts, and updates our systems. This means fewer delays at distribution centers. Figure 8.8 shows a robot handling invoices [2].

Figure 8.8 A robot handling invoices [2].

- *Supply and Demand Planning:* Anticipating and reacting to the supply and demand process can be a daunting task, especially if you just rely on human labor. Supply and demand planning relies heavily on accurate and timely data. Companies must accurately forecast customer demand and ensure the inventory supply meets the forecast targets. Accuracy is key here. And for accuracy, we need reliable data. Before automation, supply and demand planning were a tedious process. This is where RPA comes in. With smart bots, companies can collect, store, and extract crucial data needed for accurate forecasting. The bot can collect data from anywhere - any system, emails, market intelligence reports, sales teams, vendor data, and so on, to provide the most accurate picture of the current climate.

- *Shipment Tracking*: Automation is used to track shipments in real time. AI and IoT tools help us see where parcels move from our distribution centers to last-mile delivery spots. A logistics provider raised shipment tracking accuracy by 95% using robotic process automation. This helps us fix bottlenecks fast and keep customers happy. Order management becomes faster as we analyze data and spot delays before they become big problems. Automation improved our shipment tracking accuracy by ninety-five percent.

- *Logistics and Transportation:* Shipping the products to the right destination is also a very crucial part of supply chain management. Transportation companies play a critical role in the supply chain. They deliver goods across different links, including material suppliers, manufacturers, retailers, and customers. Logistics and transportation are integral elements of the supply chain, involving the movement and management of goods from suppliers to customers. Efficient tracking and route optimization are crucial for minimizing costs, enhancing delivery speed, and improving overall operational efficiency. Traffic jams, bad weather, and other events that cause unexpected delays no longer need to bring transportation and logistics to a standstill, thanks to automation. RPA simplifies and accelerates the tracking of shipments and management of transportation logistics. RPA bots can automate tasks such as updating shipment statuses or generating tracking reports. Artificial intelligence (AI) enhances route optimization by analyzing a wide range of data to determine the most efficient delivery routes. Companies like UPS have turned logistics into an art form, using smart technology to cut down delivery times and optimize the basics of every trip.

- *Predictive Maintenance:* Predictive maintenance is an advanced approach to equipment upkeep that leverages data and technology to anticipate and address potential failures before they occur. Traditionally, maintenance activities were reactive or scheduled at fixed intervals, often leading to unnecessary downtime or unexpected breakdowns. RPA and AI enhance the efficiency of maintenance workflows by automating various tasks associated with maintenance management. RPA can handle administrative tasks such as generating maintenance work orders, tracking inventory of spare parts, and updating maintenance records.

8.5 Benefits

RPA can greatly improve business process automation, which will increase accuracy, productivity, and efficiency. It automates jobs and frees up human resources to concentrate on more crucial operations. It makes quick data exchange possible, increasing processing effectiveness. By enabling workers to concentrate on more strategic responsibilities, RPA improves job satisfaction and raises employee satisfaction. Automation improves transparency. Other benefits of RPA in the supply chain include the following [11,14,15]:

- *Cost Reduction:* Given all the advantages, robotic process automation is economical because it reduces audit expenses, speeds up process cycle times, gets rid of errors, and increases productivity. By removing errors, speeding up process cycle times, improving productivity, improving decision-making, workforce optimization, and business process scaling, RPA helps reduce operational costs. RPA systems effectively perform tasks, thereby minimizing the likelihood of errors and eliminating the necessity for repetitive human actions. Consequently, this accelerates task completion and lowers costs, as there is no requirement to hire additional team members for task execution. By simplifying audit procedures, robotic process automation can lower audit expenses.
- *Customer Service:* Customer service is a critical touchpoint in the supply chain, especially when it comes to post-sale support. RPA helps streamline this area by automating tasks like processing returns and issuing refunds. RPA can help field customer inquiries, solve issues, and educate customers. As a result, your clients will have their problems handled faster, questions answered in a more timely manner, and ultimately, a much-improved customer experience.
- *Customer Satisfaction:* Customer satisfaction provides another vital measure of RPA's effectiveness, reflecting improvements in service speed, order accuracy, and communication transparency. RPA revolutionizes customer communication by automating updates through SMS or email. This keeps customers well-informed and reduces the workload on customer service teams. As a result, they can focus on more

complex tasks, thereby improving the overall service experience.

- *Enhanced Accuracy:* Human errors in data entry and manual processing can lead to major disruptions. RPA eliminates these errors by automating data handling, which ensures consistent and accurate records across the supply chain. It enhances the precision of supply chain operations. Automating tasks prone to human error, like order management and inventory control, ensures accurate data handling. This 24/7 operational reliability drastically reduces mistakes, creating a more trustworthy and efficient supply chain environment.
- *Increased Efficiency:* When it comes to efficiency, RPA is a game-changer. Supply chain managers typically juggle numerous time-consuming tasks. RPA enables businesses to automate time-consuming tasks such as inventory updates, order processing, and demand planning. RPA applications work at a faster rate, cutting down data management time by up to 50%. This significant reduction in workload leads to enhanced overall business efficiency. RPA reduces human labor by using bots to automate operations across several systems and applications, hence improving operational efficiency.
- *Increased Visibility:* Limited visibility into supply chain operations hinders decision-making. RPA can collect and process data from various systems, providing real-time insights into supply chain performance. Enhanced visibility helps identify potential issues and take proactive measures.
- *Enhanced Decision Making:* RPA can collect and process data to generate predictive insights, helping businesses anticipate future trends. By combining RPA with advanced analytics,

organizations can optimize decision-making and identify the best course of action.

- *Data Entry:* Data entry is a critical part of supply chain operations, but it is also prone to errors and delays. Supply chains generate massive amounts of data, from purchase orders and invoices to shipping manifests and customs declarations. Manually entering and managing this data is not only tedious but also prone to errors. RPA can automatically extract and input data from invoices, orders, and shipping documents, ensuring that all records are up-to-date and accurate. RPA bots can extract data from emails, PDFs, spreadsheets, and web portals, and then validate and input it into the appropriate systems. This ensures that records are accurate, up to date, and accessible across departments.
- *Data Analytics*: Data analytics is critical to supply chain automation, as it turns raw data into actionable insights predicting demand, optimizing inventory, and identifying inefficiencies. By analyzing large volumes of data from various sources across the supply chain, companies can identify patterns that can inform decision-making.
- *Scalability:* Scalability metrics assess how well RPA adapts to increased workloads or new workflows, demonstrating its ability to grow alongside business needs. RPA is a great solution in supply chain management, and it enables a business to scale up fast. During peak seasons or sudden spikes in demand, businesses can scale their bot workforce easily without significant costs or infrastructure changes. This flexibility is a key advantage in dynamic markets. Because robotic process automation may scale up or down without adding more workers, it improves scalability potential in response to changing volumes.

Some of these benefits are displayed in Figure 8.9 [14].

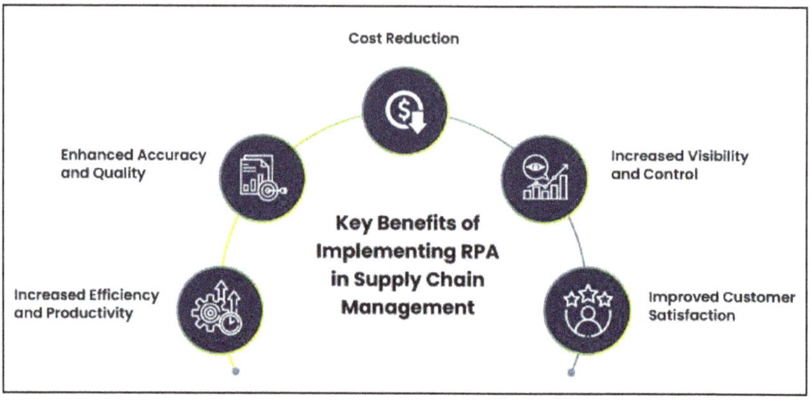

Figure 8.9 Some of these benefits of RPA [14].

8.6 Challenges

Finding processes that can be automated is a hurdle in robotic process automation. Not every process can be automated via robotic process automation. Determining which procedures stand to gain from automation is crucial. For software robots to function properly, all tasks must have explicit instructions. Workers have too much information to retain. High costs often stand in the way. Many companies face trouble integrating RPA with their current systems. RPA software is not a way to automate skilled labor out of the job. Other challenges of RPA in supply chain include the following [11,16,17]:

- *Implementation Costs*: Technology and infrastructure costs at the onset can be high. The cost of RPA varies depending on the scale and requirements of the organization. Small and medium-sized enterprises might incur expenses ranging from

$4,000 to $15,000 for a single bot. Large enterprise organizations may invest up to $20 million for a comprehensive RPA solution comprising up to 500 robots. Such a deployment has the potential to replace over 1,000 employees and yield savings exceeding $100 million.

- *Legacy Systems:* Each organization has its own legacy systems, multiple data inputs, and manual processes. The ability to connect significantly dissimilar systems across your supply chain allows you to have more data on hand faster when making executive decisions about forecasting, while ensuring your demand planning is accurate. RPA integrates seamlessly with a variety of supply chain management systems, including commercial, off-the-shelf solutions as well as homegrown, custom platforms
- *Order Processing Delays*: Order processing often involves manual tasks such as data entry, order verification, and inventory checks, which can lead to delays and errors. RPA can automate the entire order-to-fulfillment process, ensuring that orders are processed quickly and accurately, and reducing lead times.
- *Inventory Management Inefficiencies*: Maintaining accurate inventory records can be challenging, particularly when dealing with large volumes of goods. RPA can automatically update inventory systems in real time, ensuring that stock levels are always accurate and that inventory is replenished when needed.
- *Shipment Tracking:* Keeping track of shipments and providing timely updates to customers can be a complex task. RPA can automate the tracking of shipments, providing real-time

updates and notifying customers of delays or changes in delivery schedules.

- *Data Quality:* AI systems depend on good-quality data; bad data can result in poor-quality insights and decisions that are not optimal.
- *Data Security*: Data security is another big concern for us. We need to protect sensitive information while using new technology like AI or IoT tools.
- *Change Management:* Managing changes is a difficult task for any organization. It requires a lot of time and effort. Changes are needed, but risks linger as we adapt to these challenges in our operations. Organizations need to manage the shift to automated systems with caution to ensure acceptance by employees and reduce resistance. Resistance to change can deter progress, so teams shifting to automation need to receive plenty of advance notice and clear communication about how to execute the plan.
- *Regulatory Compliance:* Regulations are constantly changing, making it difficult for companies to keep up. The automation of supply chain processes significantly minimizes the likelihood of mistakes that could jeopardize a company's ability to maintain regulatory compliance and provide detailed audit trails. Systems can track and log every step of product handling so safety and legal standards are met without extra effort. This reduces the risk of compliance issues and fines while also giving companies peace of mind that they're following all the rules. Designed well, automation can also improve compliance in another critical area: the heightening regulatory oversight of environmental and social responsibility in supply chains.

8.7 Future Of Robotic Process Automation In Supply Chain

RPA in the supply chain automates repetitive tasks like inventory tracking, order processing, and shipment scheduling. As technology continues to evolve, RPA will play an increasingly important role in shaping the future of supply chain management. By embracing these trends, organizations can gain a competitive advantage and drive operational excellence. As the supply chain landscape continues to evolve, RPA will play an increasingly crucial role in shaping the future of logistics. AI and IoT are becoming key players in this space since these technologies help us analyze data more effectively. The future of supply chain management is the increasing fusion of these technologies and RPA. The combination of RPA and AI facilitates seamless coordination between different components of the supply chain. While RPA is great at following rules, combining it with artificial intelligence takes automation to the next level. This blend, often called intelligent automation, allows bots to make decisions, learn from data, and adapt to changing conditions.

In the future, supply chains are expected to become more agile, transparent, and responsive, allowing companies to operate with increasing levels of precision and efficiency. Robotics will continue to take center stage in warehousing, with machines handling a variety of complex tasks—such as sorting, packing, assembling, and distributing products. The rise of autonomous vehicles and drones is a major development that will affect the supply chain. These technologies could transform supply chain logistics, making deliveries significantly quicker and more cost-effective.

8.8 Conclusion

Because automation helps companies do more with less, it can be especially advantageous for curbing the potential effects of rising material costs, limited warehouse space, and fluctuating transportation costs. Automation not only increases the efficiency of supply chains, but it creates resilience, allowing companies to pivot in the face of uncertainty to stay ahead of changing market conditions. Automation also helps companies respond to increasingly common supply chain disruptions.

Robotic process automation (RPA) in the supply chain involves using software robots to automate repetitive, rules-based tasks like data entry, order processing, and inventory management. RPA can change how we manage the supply chain. It has the potential to revolutionize supply chain management by automating repetitive tasks, improving accuracy, and driving efficiency. It transforms supply chain management by automating repetitive tasks, reducing errors, and improving overall efficiency. Many companies see RPA as essential for success in this sector.

Although RPA is in the early stages of adoption within supply chain operations, businesses are rapidly embracing automation to streamline and enhance the efficiency of their supply chains. Organizations that embrace automation now will not only gain operational efficiency but also build a more intelligent and future-ready supply chain ecosystem. Although we will see supply chain disruption for the next several years, we do not need to resign ourselves to defeat. More information about robotic process automation in the supply chain can be found in the books [18-20] and a related journal: *Supply Chain Analytics.*

References

[1] "How robotic process automation (RPA) is optimizing 'business-as-usual'" August 2021,

https://medium.com/elucidate-ai/how-robotic-process-automation-rpa-is-optimizing-business-as-usual-1c5e5c46ef43

[2] J. S. M. Falcon, "RPA uses for supply chain management,"

https://www.smartflow.ie/post/rpa-uses-for-supply-chain-management

[3] M. N. O. Sadiku, S. A. Ajayi, and J. O. Sadiku, "Robotic process automation in supply chain," *International Journal of Trend in Scientific Research and Development*, vol. 10, no. 1, January-February, 2026, pp. 697-706.

[4] N. Komitsky, "Putting robotic process automation to work in the federal government,"

https://www.managementconcepts.com/resource/putting-robotic-process-automation-to-work-in-the-federal-government/

[5] "What is robotic process automation (RPA)? how it works?" February 2023,

https://solidpro-es.com/what-is-robotic-process-automation-rpa-how-it-works/

[6] F. Caltin, "RPA in finance," February 2020,

https://www.plutushealthinc.com/post/rpa-in-finance

[7] "Absolutely everything you need to know about robotic process automation,"

https://www.blueprism.com/guides/robotic-process-automation-rpa/

[8] S. Donnelly, "5 Benefits of robotic process automation in finance," September 2022,

https://www.financealliance.io/5-benefits-of-robotic-process-automation-in-finance/

[9] "Robotic process automation in finance," September 2023,

https://kmbs.konicaminolta.us/blog/robotic-process-automation-in-finance/

[10] "Robotic process automation in finance,"

https://planergy.com/blog/robotic-process-automation-finance/

https://www.uipath.com/resources/automation-whitepapers/robotic-process-automation-in-telecommunications-csps

[11] "RPA in supply chain: Revolutionizing logistics,"

https://innowise.com/blog/rpa-in-supply-chain/

[12] C. Pierce, "Top 5 use cases for automation in supply chain management in 2023,"

https://www.thoughtful.ai/blog/top-5-use-cases-for-automating-supply-chains-in-2023

[13] "5 Examples of supply chain automation with RPA and AI for greater efficiency and cost reduction," https://gleematic.com/5-examples-of-supply-chain-automation-with-rpa-and-ai-for-greater-efficiency-and-cost-reduction/

[14] Charter Global, "Robotic process automation: How RPA is driving supply chain efficiency and cost savings," August 2024,

https://www.charterglobal.com/rpa-supply-chain-automation/

[15] A. Shamsuzzoha and S. Pelkonen, "A robotic process automation model for order-handling optimization in supply chain management," *Supply Chain Analytics*, vol. 9, March 2025.

[16] "Supply chain & logistics automation with RPA,"

https://www.keyence.com/products/software/rpa/departments/supply-chain-logistics.jsp

[17] A. Mancini, "How robotic process automation is used in supply chains,"July 2025, https://www.impactmybiz.com/blog/how-robotic-process-automation-is-used-supply-chains/

[18] B. Nitsche, *Exploring the Potentials of Automation in Logistics and Supply Chain Management: Paving the Way for Autonomous Supply Chains*. Mdpi AG, 2021.

[19] B. Galińska and M. Stachura, *Robotic Process Automation Technology in Supply Chain Management: Practical Applications for Simplifying Workflows*. Taylor & Francis, 2025.

[20] Nikola, *Optimizing Operations: Harnessing Robotic Process Automation for Supply Chain Success.* Sunshine, 2023.

CHAPTER 9
ROBOTIC PROCESS AUTOMATION IN LOGISTICS

"Tell me, and I forget. Teach me, and I remember. Involve me, and I learn."

Benjamin Franklin

9.1 Introduction

As consumer demand for faster and more reliable delivery and transparency continues to rise, the integration of advanced robotic systems has become increasingly essential for companies striving to maintain a competitive edge. There are two types of robots: hardware and software. Hardware (physical) robots have a tangible material structure and perform physical tasks in a variety of environments. Software (virtual) robots operate entirely in a digital environment and consist of machine algorithms that mimic humans. The most common type of software robot is robotic process automation (RPA) [1]. By automating repetitive tasks, RPA facilitates enhanced accuracy and speed, enabling companies to manage their supply chain logistics more effectively. In the logistics sector, where precision and speed are paramount, RPA has found its niche. Figure 9.1 provides a definition of robotic process automation [2], while Figure 9.2 shows some logistics professionals [3].

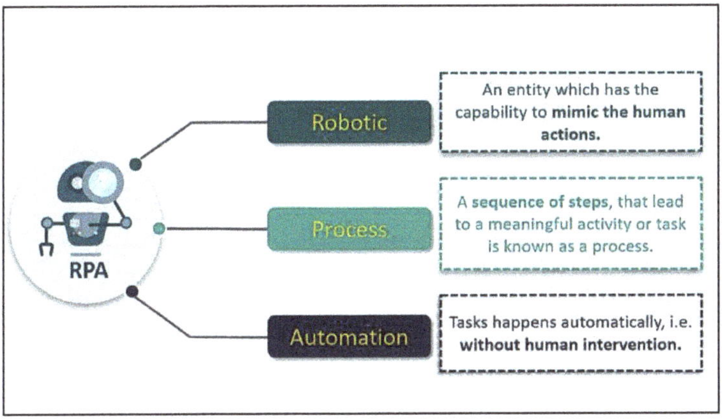

Figure 9.1 A definition of robotic process automation [2].

Figure 9.2 Some logistics professionals [3].

The influence of automation on global trade is expanding as industries aim to enhance operational efficiency. In the era of digital transformation, robotic process automation (RPA) has emerged as a pivotal technology for enhancing operational efficiency and sustainability in logistics. RPA involves the use of software robots to automate repetitive tasks, reducing human intervention and the potential for errors. RPA in logistics helps automate routine activities like manual data entry, shipment tracking, and delivery scheduling. By automating routine and repetitive tasks, RPA reduces human error, accelerates process execution, and significantly lowers energy consumption in both warehouse and transportation logistics [4].

The primary goal of this chapter is to explore the potential impact of RPA on logistics processes. The chapter begins with explaining the concept of robotic process automation (RPA). It describes RPA in logistics and provides some of its applications. It highlights the benefits and challenges of RPA in logistics. It predicts the future of RPA in logistics. The last section concludes with comments.

9.2 What Is Robotic Process Automation?

The term “robotic process automation” (RPA) appeared relatively recently, but the phenomenon itself has been around for a long time. Among the various forms of artificial intelligence, RPA stands out for its potential to significantly increase workforce productivity by reducing or eliminating the need to do repetitive tasks manually. Popular applications of RPA include data entry, data reconciliation, spreadsheet manipulation, systems integration, automated data reporting, analytics, email notifications, acquisitions, administrative services, finance, human resources, mission assurance, strategic communications, travel reimbursements, claims processing, and customer outreach and communications. These are just a few examples of the ways RPA is being used to remove the burden of manual, repetitive, and duplicative tasks from public service workers [5].

Robotic process automation is a form of automation software. It is a technology that can automate repetitive, rules-based tasks. Like an Excel macro operating within a spreadsheet, RPA can record actions performed across a personal computer, access systems, and perform specific tasks for human users. It uses software robots, more commonly called “bots,” that mimic basic human-computer interactions. Figure 9.3 shows the symbol of RPA [6], while Figure 9.4 shows processes that RPA can automate [7]. Most industries use RPA. The government does too. Due to the repetitive nature of some tasks, the probability of human error increases. One way to eliminate errors is by using RPA. Robotic process automation solutions fall into three key categories: attended RPA, unattended RPA, and hybrid RPA, as shown in Figure 9.5 [8].

Figure 9.3 Symbol of RPA [6].

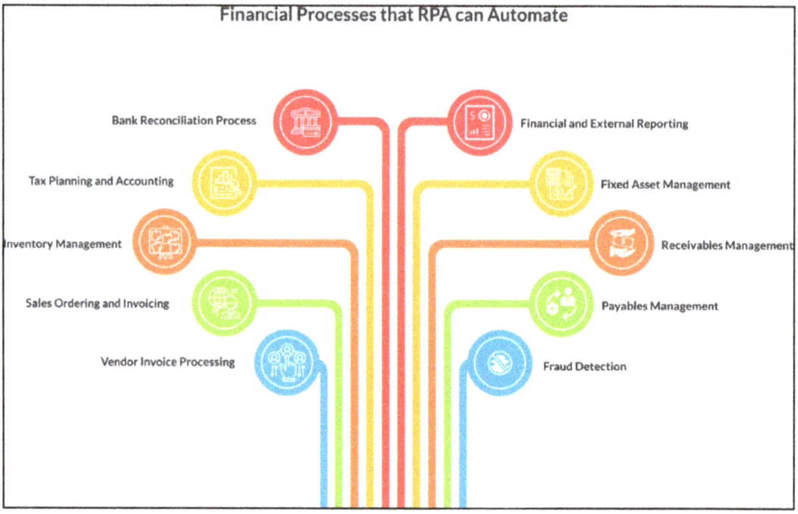

Figure 9.4 Processes that RPA can automate [7].

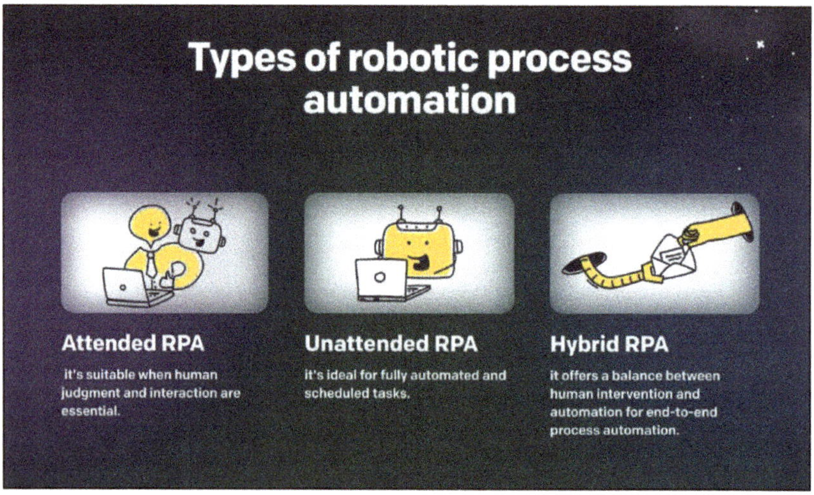

Figure 9.5 Three types of RPA [8].

Robotic process automation is a type of software that mimics the activity of a human being in carrying out a task within a process. It is a technology that automates repetitive tasks using software robots. RPA uses a set of automation tools to automate repetitive tasks and manual processes performed electronically. Since RPA can automate tasks that are rule-based, manual, repetitive, and tedious, delivering the highest levels of accuracy and eradicating human errors, it is a seamless fit for the finance industry. Here are some specific examples of what RPA in finance can do [9]:

- Opening emails and joining attachments
- Automatically logging into various applications on the web
- Shifting folders and files
- Copying and pasting
- Completing forms
- Collecting data from databases and the web
- Making calculations
- Connecting to system API
- Extracting structured data from documents
- Gathering stats from social media
- Following if/then decisions and rules

Some of these tasks are displayed in Figure 9.6 [8].

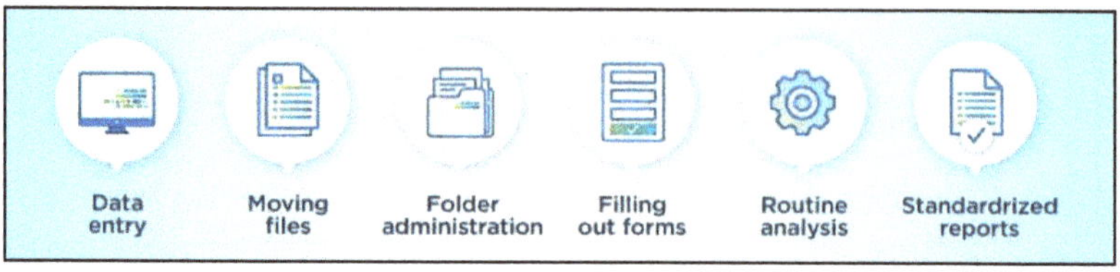

Figure 9.6 Some tasks RPA can perform [8].

At its core, robotic process automation (RPA) is a tool designed to mimic rule-based business processes, performing them seamlessly and without fatigue. RPA is a rule-driven method that is limited in its application. The technology functions much like a Microsoft Excel macro; the key difference is in power and reach. It follows set rules, similar to how an Excel macro works, to do things like move files or log into accounts. Growing as a popular solution in finance and accounting, RPA refers to software technology or "software robots" with artificial intelligence (AI) and machine learning (ML) capabilities. The "software robots" have the ability to learn and complete a high volume of rules-based, repetitive tasks and business processes. They have the capacity to operate much faster than humans, with 100% precision and reliability, working around the clock.

Finance and human resources are just two examples of departments likely to have many use cases that RPA can help solve. Some examples of good use cases for RPA in finance include processing customer orders, ensuring timely vendor payments, and managing period-end financial close processes. For human resources, some examples include employee onboarding, time tracking, and leave of absence management. Processes where human judgment is needed are not appropriate for RPA since RPA automations rely on clear, consistently applied rules [10].

Along with RPA, one should be aware of both business process automation (BPA) and digital process automation (DPA) – two commonly used automation technologies that robotics process automation can be paired with to optimize and streamline a digital transformation. BPA refers to the use of technology to automate complex, multi-step workflows, typically very specific to a company's core business functions. DPA offers dual power by automating processes from end to end and optimizing common workflows that involve external human interactions (i.e., sales, management). Separately, RPA and AI are quite powerful, but leveraging them together is undoubtedly advantageous to any financial institution. When deployed together, AI is the "brains" behind RPA's bots [11].

9.3 Robotic Process Automation In Logistics

Logistics has undergone significant change in recent years due to technological advancements, increasing customer expectations, and global challenges. It is a critical part of economic growth as it enables businesses to expand globally and make their presence in the international market. It is one of the many domains of interest for RPA implementation. Logistics is characterized not only by physical processes but also by digital processes such as interactions between application systems that can potentially be automated with RPA.

The digital transformation of logistics, driven by AI, ML, and robotics, offers a rich array of research opportunities for business researchers, particularly in the area of resource orchestration. Resource orchestration in logistics refers to how companies strategically manage and coordinate the deployment of AI, robotics, and automation to optimize workflows, enhance efficiency, and adapt to dynamic market conditions. The emergence of innovative robotics in logistics and supply chain management has transformed the way businesses operate, enhancing accuracy and speed in a highly competitive and digitalized global market. The concept of using automation in logistics dates back to the early 20th century with the advent of conveyor belts and automated sorting systems. The adoption of RPA in logistics is outpacing other sectors, with nearly 25% of companies having already implemented these technologies in their logistics operations.

9.4 Applications Of Robotic Process Automation In Logistics

The logistics function consists of some processes that managers adjust to enhance agility. These include forecasting, demand planning, sourcing, procurement, inbound transportation, warehousing, and outbound transportation. Common application areas of RPA in logistics include the following [12-14]:

- *Logistics Robots:* The advancement of artificial intelligence and machine learning technologies is a key element driving the adoption of robotics in logistics. Organizations are increasingly integrating robotics into their logistics processes. Robotics in logistics represents a transformative force that is revolutionizing how goods are transported, stored, and managed. It involves the use of automated machines and systems to perform tasks traditionally handled by human labor. These tasks include sorting, picking, packing, transporting, and inventory management. The integration of robotics into logistics processes has led to significant improvements in efficiency, accuracy, and cost-effectiveness. RPA robots are very accurate and make zero mistakes when working with data. Amazon has invested heavily in robotic technology, such as its Amazon Robotics. These robots move entire shelves of products to human workers, rather than workers having to walk through large warehouses to pick items. Figure 9.7 shows how robots work in a warehouse [13].

Figure 9.7 How robots work in a warehouse [13].

- *Logistics Automation:* Automation of logistics processes, and even entire production lines, is becoming a global trend. Logistics automation is the application of computer software or automated machinery to logistics operations in order to improve their efficiency. By using automation, a company can spend less money on operations. This means that tasks get done quicker, so the current employees can do other important jobs, and the company does not have to hire new people. RPA in automation simplifies freight documentation, tariff calculations, and customs compliance, making cross-border movement smoother while reducing the scope for manual errors. The application of automation also helps improve customer service. Everything happens faster with RPA in automation, so customers can order things and get them quicker than before. A complete warehouse automation system can drastically reduce the workforce required to run a facility, with human input required only for a few tasks, such as picking units of product from a bulk-packed case. Automation Anywhere offers flexible deployment options and is aimed primarily at large enterprises, although it is also reaching out to midsize businesses. It emphasizes ease of use with its scriptless automation approach, allowing users without programming skills to automate processes.
- *Order Processing:* In logistics, order processing involves many repetitive activities, including accepting orders from multiple channels, validating customer details, generating invoices, and updating order statuses. These tasks can be time-consuming and error-prone if performed manually. With RPA in automation, order processing becomes a breeze. RPA can help streamline order processing, enabling companies to fulfill more orders and speed up deliveries. Robots can validate

orders, process invoices, and even prepare shipments, minimizing the chances of discrepancies and delays.

- *Shipment Tracking:* Errors in shipment scheduling and tracking can lead to delayed deliveries and misrouted shipments, undermining customer trust and incurring additional costs. Companies can use RPA tools to track shipments in real-time and quickly take necessary actions in case of delays or other issues. RPA tools can also track shipping statuses for orders and automatically send notifications to customers with updates, improving transparency and helping build trust with customers.
- *Warehouse Automation*: One of the most prominent applications of robotics in logistics is warehouse automation. Warehouses are the heart of logistics, and RPA serves as a reliable heartbeat. With RPA, companies can automate multiple warehouse management activities, minimizing travel time within the warehouse and maximizing throughput. Warehouse managers can also use bots to automatically assign tasks to specific workers based on item location, worker availability, and delivery urgency, minimizing the time needed to pick the item and increasing staff productivity.
- *Customer Service:* Customer service teams can use bots to respond to general customer queries. With bots operating 24/7 and providing multilingual support, companies can significantly reduce query processing times for the team and waiting times for customers. By adopting RPA to handle routine customer-facing tasks, companies free up more time for their sales reps and support agents to build stronger relationships with clients.

- *Inventory Management:* Maintaining optimal inventory levels is critical for companies that heavily rely on logistics, like retailers or manufacturers, to prevent disruptions in supply chains and effectively meet customer demand. Robots equipped with advanced sensors and AI capabilities are used for inventory management. RPA is adept at handling inventory-related tasks, from tracking stock levels to generating real-time reports. RPA tools can run real-time inventory checks for item availability and alert relevant teams or automatically place new orders when stock levels drop below a certain limit. This helps prevent understocking and streamlines order fulfillment.

9.5 Benefits

The benefits of RPA in logistics are manifold. Organizations profit from a fast and reliably predictable return on investment. Further benefits are the increasing process execution speed and 24/7 availability of bots, as well as higher process execution accuracy and improved compliance due to log data transparency. More complex areas of logistics, such as supplier risk and compliance management, can soon be facilitated by RPA bots in collaboration with AI and machine learning. Other benefits include the following [12]:

- *Lower Operational Costs:* Due to minimized human intervention and bots' 24/7 availability, companies can speed up task completion while cutting labor expenses and eliminating inefficiencies in processes. The automation of routine tasks enables employees to conduct more value-adding work and coincides with cost reductions achieved by workforce salary savings.

- *Higher Productivity*: By automating repetitive, time-consuming tasks, RPA allows employees to devote their time to tasks requiring human judgment and add more value.
- *Increased Customer Satisfaction:* RPA enables companies to fulfill orders faster, increase shipment visibility, and provide accurate data to customers, which helps foster their trust and loyalty.
- *Increased Employee Satisfaction:* When RPA is used, employees are happier and more likely to stay in their jobs. This is because they can focus on important things like making decisions, coming up with new ideas, talking to other companies, and helping the business grow. This makes them feel good about their work. RPA helps employees do their work better.
- *Regulatory Compliance:* Adhering to legal and compliance standards is a nonnegotiable facet of RPA deployment. Organizations must meticulously align their automation strategies with the pertinent regulatory requirements and legal obligations, ensuring that operational enhancements do not come at the expense of compliance. Companies from the logistics industry must comply with multiple transportation safety, customs, and environmental regulations, and RPA solutions can assist in meeting these requirements. For example, software robots can generate error-free shipping documents, customs declarations, and other official forms, minimizing the risk of compliance errors and penalties.

9.6 Challenges

Like any other technology, adopting RPA can entail various challenges. Although RPA has been regarded as a trendy technology on the market, resources for high-level deployment and implementation from RPA as a service remain underexplored. Since RPA is a relatively new technology, it faces barriers similar to those for other enabling technologies, such as the lack of knowledge about data management. Human-intensive operations can be error-prone. Other challenges include the following [15]:

- *Implementation Cost*: The cost of implementing RPA is a top barrier to its deployment for logistics management. The initial investment in robotic systems can be high, which may be a barrier for small and medium-sized enterprises (SMEs). However, the long-term benefits often outweigh the costs, leading to a positive return on investment.
- *Ethical Concerns:* In using RPA, stringent data privacy and security measures are imperative to protect against unauthorized data access and breaches, ensuring confidentiality and integrity. The practice of circumventing costs through RPA, particularly to avoid data usage fees, raises significant ethical concerns, potentially infringing on contractual obligations and intellectual property rights. The increasing use of robots in logistics raises ethical and social concerns, such as job displacement and the need for workforce reskilling. Companies must address these issues by investing in employee training and creating new job opportunities in robot maintenance and management.

- *Transparency:* Transparency in the usage of RPA is equally critical, necessitating the establishment of explicit policies that delineate the scope and modalities of RPA operations, ensuring that stakeholders have a clear understanding of the governance mechanisms in place.
- *Employee Resistance:* Employees can be reluctant to adopt the new technology, fearing they can lose their jobs or refusing to give up familiar workflows. To popularize RPA implementation in the logistics industry, potential functional and psychological barriers derived from the innovation resistance should be considered.
- *Lack of Knowledge:* It is important to note that RPA technology cannot be used if supply chain members lack knowledge about data management. To allow the automated handling of data exchange by RPA, all parties need to be familiar with technological requirements and features. Small or medium-sized enterprises lacking human resources and no expansion goals may find it difficult to digitalize.
- *Integration:* The chosen RPA platform should integrate seamlessly with existing business systems, including enterprise resource planning, order management systems, warehouse management systems, transportation management systems, and other legacy systems.
- *Engagement:* Engaging stakeholders is an indispensable part of this ecosystem, fostering an environment where feedback and concerns regarding the RPA deployment are actively solicited and addressed. This engagement not only enhances the acceptance of RPA solutions but also reinforces the ethical fabric of its application, ensuring that the deployment of such

technologies is congruent with the broader organizational values and societal norms.

9.7 Future Of Robotic Process Automation In Logistics

As the logistics and supply chain industry continues to evolve, the role of RPA will likely grow in significance. With organizations prioritizing logistics and inventory management, the integration of RPA tools is expected to provide substantial benefits, from increased efficiency to improved decision-making capabilities. The future is promising. Incorporating RPA in logistics enhances accuracy, accelerates operations, and paves the way for a more efficient and cost-effective future in the logistics industry. We can expect RPA to become even more intelligent and adaptable, revolutionizing logistics operations.

9.8 Conclusion

Robotic process automation (RPA) involves using software robots to automate repetitive tasks that were previously performed by humans. It eliminates the risk of human error, ensuring precise execution of tasks like order processing, inventory management, and data entry. The integration of robotics in supply chains is a fundamental shift in how organizations execute their supply chain logistics.

The RPA market is mature, with dozens of software vendors offering both universal and niche products for task automation. As RPA tools become more prevalent, they are set to reshape the logistics and supply chain management landscape, offering new opportunities for growth and innovation. RPA has the potential to increase quality and efficiency. More information about robotic process automation in logistics can be found in the book [16] and a related journal: *Journal of Business Logistics.*

References

[1] R. K. Rainer, R. G. Richey, and S. Chowdhury, "How robotics is shaping digital logistics and supply chain management: An ongoing call for research," *Journal of Business Logistics*, January 2025

[2] "How robotic process automation (RPA) is optimizing 'business-as-usual'" August 2021, https://medium.com/elucidate-ai/how-robotic-process-automation-rpa-is-optimizing-business-as-usual-1c5e5c46ef43

[3] https://images.search.yahoo.com/search/images?p=images+of+logistics+professionals&fr=mcafee&type=E210US1357G0&imgurl=https%3A%2F%2Fwww.thebusinessconcept.com%2Fwp-content%2Fuploads%2F2023%2F02%2FLogistics-Career.jpg#id=9&iurl=https%3A%2F%2Fwww.thebusinessconcept.com%2Fwp-content%2Fuploads%2F2023%2F02%2FLogistics-Career.jpg&action=click

[4] M. N. O. Sadiku and J. O. Sadiku, "Robotic process automation in logistics," *International Journal of Trend in Research and Development,* vol. 13, no. 1, January-February 2026, pp. 130-134.

[5] N. Komitsky, "Putting robotic process automation to work in the federal government,"

https://www.managementconcepts.com/resource/putting-robotic-process-automation-to-work-in-the-federal-government/

[6] "What is robotic process automation (RPA)? How does it work?" February 2023,

https://solidpro-es.com/what-is-robotic-process-automation-rpa-how-it-works/

[7] F. Caltin, "RPA in finance," February 2020,

https://www.plutushealthinc.com/post/rpa-in-finance

[8] W. Masternak, "A closer look at robotic process automation in customer support,"

https://www.helpdesk.com/learn/robotic-process-automation/

[9] S. Donnelly, "5 Benefits of robotic process automation in finance," September 2022,

https://www.financealliance.io/5-benefits-of-robotic-process-automation-in-finance/

[10] "Robotic process automation in finance," September 2023,

https://kmbs.konicaminolta.us/blog/robotic-process-automation-in-finance/

[11] "Robotic process automation in finance,"

https://planergy.com/blog/robotic-process-automation-finance/

https://www.uipath.com/resources/automation-whitepapers/robotic-process-automation-in-telecommunications-csps

[12] V. Poleshuk, “RPA in logistics: Use cases, benefits & implementation guide,”

March 2025,

https://www.itransition.com/rpa/logistics

[13] “Robotics in logistics,”

https://www.discoverengineering.org/robotics-in-logistics/

[14] D. Chindarkar, “Robotic process automation in logistics,” December 2023,

https://blog.werqlabs.com/2023/12/06/robotic-process-automation-in-logistics/

[15] Y. P. Tsang et al. (eds.), “Unlocking the potential of robotic process automation for digital transformation in logistics and supply chain management,” *Journal of Global Information Management,* vol. 32, no.1, January-December 2024.

[16] B. Nitsche (ed.), *Exploring the Potentials of Automation in Logistics and Supply Chain Management: Paving the Way for Autonomous Supply Chains.* MDPI AG, 2021.

CHAPTER 10 ROBOTIC PROCESS AUTOMATION IN HUMAN RESOURCES

"Those who know how to think need no teachers."
Mahatma Gandhi

10.1 Introduction

Human resources (HR) departments, often burdened with administrative and repetitive tasks, are seeking innovative solutions to streamline operations. Robotic process automation (RPA) has emerged as a powerful tool to address these challenges by automating routine tasks, thereby freeing HR professionals to engage in more strategic activities. RPA has the potential to streamline operations, enhance employee productivity, and reshape strategic HR functions. RPA technology is often seen as a stepping stone towards broader intelligent automation, which includes artificial intelligence (AI), natural language processing (NLP), and machine learning (ML).

RPA in HR involves the deployment of software robots that perform monotonous and high-volume candidate sorting, hiring, and employment data management faster and more accurately than human workers. By automating repetitive and standardized tasks, RPA empowers HR teams to allocate more time and energy towards strategic decision-making. RPA is now regularly used within HR to automate processes such as coalescing or auditing datasets, sending offer letters to job candidates, onboarding new hires, facilitating health plan enrollment, and even creating badges for conferences and special events. RPA in HR has streamlined operations, driven efficiency, and reduced costs in human resource operations. It helps automate a wide range of repetitive tasks and allows HR professionals to provide value-driven, human-focused work. Figure 10.1 defines robotic process automation [1], while Figure 10.2 shows some HR professionals [2].

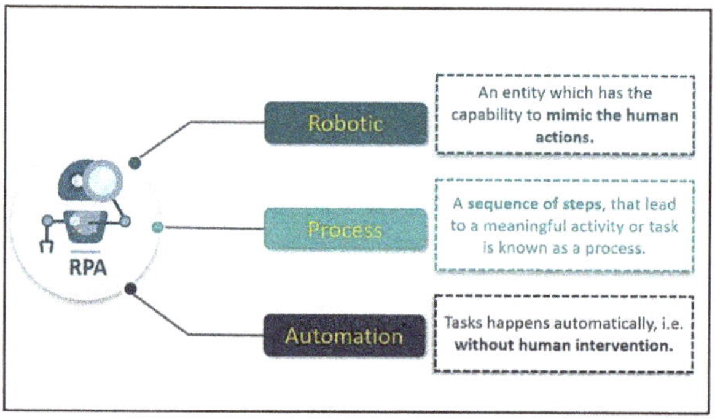

Figure 10.1 A definition of robotic process automation [1].

Figure 10.2 Some ajayHR professionals [2].

Human resources (HR) departments play a vital role in every business, taking care of each phase of an employee's life cycle, from headhunting to exit management. They can leverage robotic process automation (RPA) to streamline various activities in their daily workflow. RPA is a technology that interacts with digital systems and software to make and manage software robots. The ability to handle repetitive, high-volume tasks has made RPA an ideal tool for human resources, which traditionally handles huge amounts of paperwork. The integration of RPA within HR functions offers a transformative solution to enhance operational efficiency and elevate the role of HR professionals. The automation reduces staffing costs and human error. It promotes growth in business organization productivity, operational efficiency, and streamlining process flow [3].

This chapter emphasizes the transformative impact of robotic process automation (RPA) on human resources (HR) operations. It begins with explaining the concept of robotic process automation (RPA). It describes RPA in HR and provides some of its applications. It highlights the benefits and challenges of RPA in HR. It predicts the future of RPA in HR. The last section concludes with comments.

10.2 What Is Robotic Process Automation?

Among the various forms of artificial intelligence, RPA stands out for its potential to significantly increase workforce productivity by reducing or eliminating the need to do repetitive tasks manually.

Popular applications of RPA include data entry, data reconciliation, spreadsheet manipulation, systems integration, automated data reporting, analytics, email notifications, acquisitions, administrative services, finance, human resources, mission assurance, strategic communications, travel reimbursements, claims processing, and customer outreach and communications. These are just a few examples of the ways RPA is being used to remove the burden of manual, repetitive, and duplicative tasks from public service workers [4].

Robotic process automation is a form of automation software. It is a technology that can automate repetitive, rules-based tasks. Like an Excel macro operating within a spreadsheet, RPA can record actions performed across a personal computer, access systems, and perform specific tasks for human users. It uses software robots, more commonly called "bots," that mimic basic human-computer interactions. Figure 10.3 shows the symbol of RPA [5], while Figure 10.4 shows processes that RPA can automate [6]. Most industries use RPA. The government does too. Due to the repetitive nature of some tasks, the probability of human error increases. One way to eliminate errors is by using RPA.

Figure 10.3 Symbol of RPA [5].

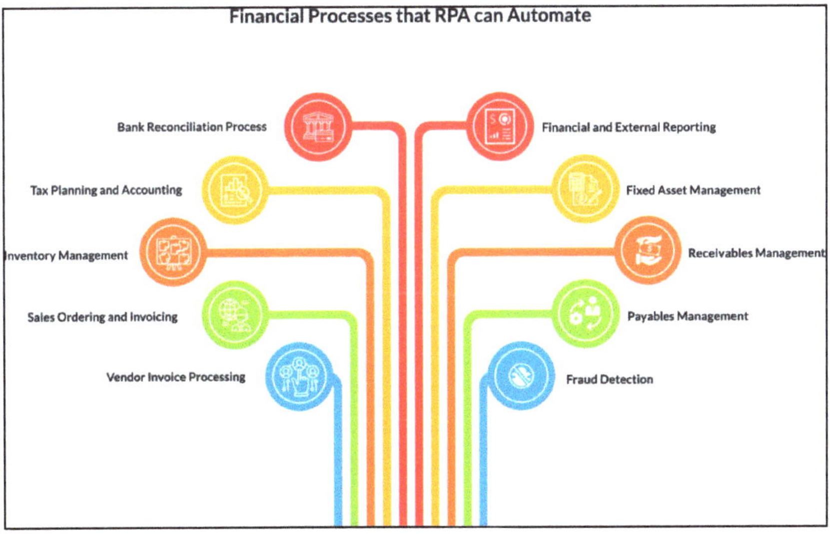

Figure 10.4 Processes that RPA can automate [6].

Robotic process automation solutions fall into three key categories: attended RPA, unattended RPA, and hybrid RPA, as shown in Figure 10.5 [7].

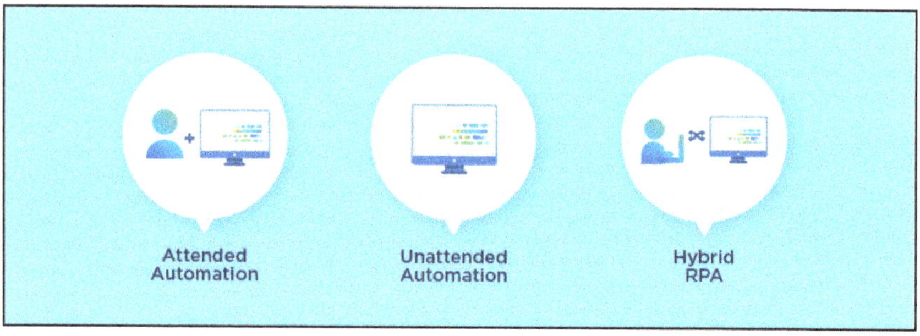

Figure 10.5 Three key categories of RPA [6].

Robotic process automation is a type of software that mimics the activity of a human being in carrying out a task within a process. It is a technology that automates repetitive tasks using software robots. RPA uses a set of automation tools to automate repetitive tasks and manual processes performed electronically. Since RPA can automate tasks that are rule-based, manual, repetitive, and tedious, delivering the highest levels of accuracy and eradicating human errors, it is a seamless fit for the finance industry. Here are some specific examples of what RPA in finance can do [8]:

- Opening emails and joining attachments
- Automatically logging into various applications on the web
- Shifting folders and files
- Copying and pasting

- Completing forms
- Collecting data from databases and the web
- Making calculations
- Connecting to system API
- Extracting structured data from documents
- Gathering stats from social media
- Following if/then decisions and rules

Some of these tasks are displayed in Figure 10.6 [7].

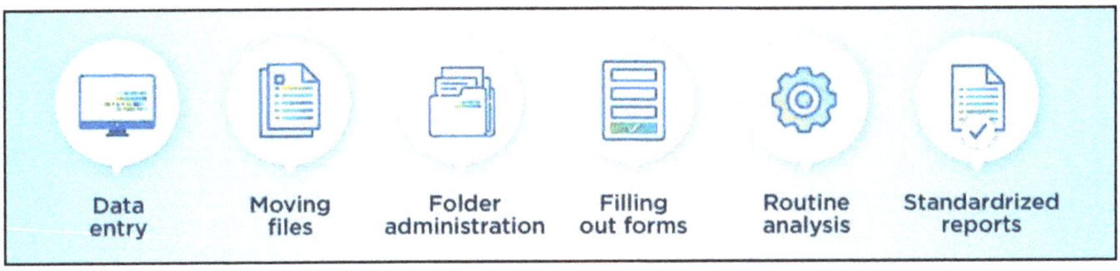

Figure 10.6 Some tasks RPA can perform [7].

At its core, robotic process automation (RPA) is a tool designed to mimic rule-based business processes, performing them seamlessly and without fatigue. RPA is a rule-driven method that is limited in its application. The technology functions much like a Microsoft Excel macro; the key difference is in power and reach. It follows set rules, similar to how an Excel macro works, to do things like move files or log into accounts. Growing as a popular solution in finance and accounting, RPA refers to software technology or "software robots" with artificial intelligence (AI) and machine learning (ML) capabilities. The "software robots" have the ability to learn and complete a high

volume of rules-based, repetitive tasks and business processes. They have the capacity to operate much faster than humans, with 100% precision and reliability, working around the clock.

Finance and human resources are just two examples of departments likely to have many use cases that RPA can help solve. Some examples of good use cases for RPA in finance include processing customer orders, ensuring timely vendor payments, and managing period-end financial close processes. For human resources, some examples include employee onboarding, time tracking, and leave of absence management. Processes where human judgment is needed are not appropriate for RPA since RPA automations rely on clear, consistently applied rules [9].

Along with RPA, one should be aware of both business process automation (BPA) and digital process automation (DPA) – two commonly used automation technologies that robotics process automation can be paired with to optimize and streamline a digital transformation. BPA refers to the use of technology to automate complex, multi-step workflows, typically very specific to a company's core business functions. DPA offers dual power by automating processes from end to end and optimizing common workflows that involve external human interactions (i.e., sales, management). Separately, RPA and AI are quite powerful, but leveraging them together is undoubtedly advantageous to any financial institution. When deployed together, AI is the "brains" behind RPA's bots [10].

10.3 Robotic Process Automation In Human Resources

Traditionally, HR functions involved manual, time-consuming tasks such as recruitment, payroll processing, employee benefits management, and performance evaluations. However, in recent years, advancements in automation technologies, specifically robotic process automation (RPA), have dramatically transformed how HR departments operate. RPA refers to the use of software robots or "bots" to automate repetitive, rule-based tasks that were previously performed by humans. A growing desire to free staff from manual tasks so they can pursue higher-value-adding work has led more HR professionals to implement RPA technology. By implementing RPA, the HR function eliminates the need for that daily time-consuming manual task. RPA has significantly transformed human resources by automating repetitive and time-consuming tasks, allowing HR professionals to focus on more strategic initiatives. Initially applied to administrative functions such as payroll, benefits management, and attendance tracking, RPA has evolved to streamline complex processes. RPA has emerged as a powerful tool that streamlines administrative processes, enhances efficiency, and reduces errors [11].

Companies should start their HR RPA program by deploying one or two bots for the most optimal low-complexity and low-risk processes. The initial low-scale automation will help measure the success of the RPA application and lay the foundation for more complex RPA solutions down the line. Once the RPA is developed and configured, integrate it with the application where the automation needs to be done. Run the automation to perform the automatic execution of the repetitive processes. Once the automation is in the live instance, the robots are available 24/7 to perform automation of various business processes. The last stage aims at testing the system and evaluating its performance in real-world conditions. During the early adoption of RPA, it is always recommended to monitor the automation as frequently as possible. Organizations must invest in upskilling and change management and ensure that RPA enhances rather than replaces the human aspect of HR [12].

10.4 Applications Of Robotic Process Automation In Human Resources

HR can use RPA to automate manual processes, standardize common tasks, quickly complete existing tasks, and free workers from the mundane to spend more time on complex projects. RPA in HR applications can range from automation to consolidation.

There are endless applications of robotic process automation in HR. Common areas of application include the following [2,13]:

- *Automation*: In the HR sector, companies have used RPA to automate a number of tasks. Companies have automated payroll updates, sick leave certification, and employee onboarding. Automation has enhanced operational efficiency, reduced costs, and improved employee and candidate experiences. Automation in the recruitment space is about far more than saving time. Email automation saves HR staff from having to manually type individual emails to respond to the large volume of messages typically received. When a hiring manager sets out the need for a new employee and sends job details and requirements, they can use RPA tools to automate job posting across a variety of websites. If you want new hires to hit the ground running, automating elements of the onboarding process is the solution. The automation of these processes has led to a streamlining of workflows and a substantial reduction in bureaucratic administrative processes into intelligent, efficient, and user-centric flows. Figure 10.7 shows the need to automate every process [14].

Figure 10.7 The need to automate every process [14].

- *Recruiting*: Sifting through a large volume of resumes and finding the ideal candidate is an uphill task. In recruiting, many tasks follow a set of predefined rules and do not require human judgment, therefore making this HR process optimal for robotic process automation. Without RPA, for example, a recruiter would have spent most, if not all, of the day sifting through resumes to find the best match, sending emails to candidates, and tracking and reporting to hiring managers the status and rationale for a hiring selection. RPA can be employed to scan and evaluate resumes against predefined criteria, shortlisting candidates whose qualifications match the job requirements. RPA software can assist in scheduling job interviews, sending out meeting invites, and, later, offer letters. In addition, RPA in recruitment helps HR departments eliminate unconscious bias, leading to more equitable candidate selection and a fair workplace.

- *Leave Management:* Logging attendance and leaves on a daily basis is quite challenging for employees, especially when it requires filling out several forms. RPA can manage employee leave requests by verifying available leave balances, cross-referencing them with the company's leave policy, planning training and events, and updating the records accordingly. It can also track attendance data and generate reports, minimizing errors and facilitating payroll processing.
- *Payroll Management:* Payroll management in HR operations involves high-volume data extraction and verification for counting working hours and considering potentially variable tax regulations. Automating payroll processes with RPA ensures accurate calculation of salaries, taxes, and deductions. The technology can extract data from timesheets, attendance records, and other sources to generate error-free payrolls, reducing the risk of human errors.
- *Employee Data Management:* Once your new hires are bedded in, there is a range of tasks that need to be done. RPA can help streamline many of these jobs. An organization's employee data management involves collecting, storing, and maintaining employee information. From employee bios and medical

information to employment details and performance data, HR requires employees to provide data about themselves. RPA can handle this data extraction from multiple systems, reduce the chances of data entry errors, and maintain accurate employee records.

- *Performance Management:* Performance management is a part of any healthy organization. HR teams need to compile a lot of data to provide accurate assessments, and RPA tools are perfect for the job of collecting data from various databases, spreadsheets, and other information sources and centralizing it for performance management reviews.

10.5 Benefits

The benefits of RPA have been recognized in HR due to the department's involvement in numerous repetitive processes, such as payroll, recruitment, and employee data management. RPA in HR operations can create a digital experience for employees and customers. Its biggest advantage is that it can liberate HR staff to use their people skills to help find solutions to pressing business problems. HR departments are turning to RPA because it is easy to implement, improves accuracy, and the tools are getting better. Other benefits include the following [15]:

- *Cost Reduction:* One of the most compelling reasons to invest in RPA is cost savings. RPA can help companies scale by augmenting their existing staff and helping them become more productive without adding new employees. RPA is adept at bridging the gap between legacy software and new tools, allowing teams to reduce the costs of investing in new tools when they have perfectly good but dated software to do the job. RPA automates key labor-intensive processes, streamlining HR operations and reducing costs.

- *Higher Efficiency*: Efficiency and accuracy are crucial in the dynamic field of human resources (HR). The traditional manual processes often struggle to keep up with the growing demand, leading to inefficiencies and errors that can affect the entire organization. Using bots, HR departments can significantly accelerate their key operations with up to 85% faster processing. Using RPA in HR operations is a surefire way to improve efficiency.
- *Increased Productivity*: Within HR, hire-to-retire refers to the entire employee lifecycle, from recruitment to onboarding to performance management right up to the point of retirement. The daily tasks of an HR professional involve a lot of repetitive, rule-based processes, like background checks, payroll adjustments, holiday authorization, performance management, resume screening, and onboarding. RPA can take on tedious administrative tasks, allowing HR staff to focus on employee engagement.
- *Increased Accuracy*: Human resources, like most other sectors and departments, have gone digital over the last few years. Communication, records, and employee data are stored digitally. With so much data going back and forth, the risk of human error has increased. The consequence of these errors could be anything from a minor inconvenience to more serious matters like work permit delays, inaccurate payments, or missing out on new hires. Enterprise RPA tools help solve these issues by eliminating human error from automated processes. Bots never get tired, which eliminates the risk of human error and ensures high data accuracy.

- *Efficient Talent Acquisition*: Talent acquisition has been a major problem within the last few years. RPA can help recruitment teams in several different ways. These tools can automate posting job ads, sifting resumes, scheduling interviews, and communicating with candidates. By streamlining the acquisition process, HR professionals have more time to focus on interviews, leading to a more efficient pipeline.
- *Scalability:* Another major benefit that using RPA for HR unlocks is the ability to scale. RPA solutions are easy to scale, so HR departments can increase the bots' operational capacity in line with their needs. RPA bots can efficiently handle payroll processing for organizations of any size, regardless of the number of employees. Sudden upturns in business can be a huge headache for HR teams as they struggle to manage new hires. However, enterprise software testing automation tools and RPA solutions can grow with you, meaning new business does not mean more strain on your HR team.
- *Employee Satisfaction:* Employee experience refers to the degree to which the employee enjoys a personalized, pleasant, and digital experience on the job. RPA is well-known for its ability to increase employee satisfaction. With no human errors and increased availability and processing time, RPA improves customer and employee satisfaction. Much of the coverage around this issue involves automating mundane tasks and allowing operatives to concentrate on more engaging and interesting jobs. By freeing up HR managers from repetitive tasks, RPA helps increase their job satisfaction and reduce staff turnover.

10.6 Challenges

The challenges of RPA implementation include employee resistance, integration with legacy systems, and concerns about job displacement. One of the major concerns of HR professionals is that technologies like RPA will eliminate their jobs. But most of the evidence to date indicates that this is unlikely. Many proponents argue that bots will improve jobs rather than replace them. However, HR is filled with a lot of transactional work that we no longer need human capability to perform. Other challenges include the following [15]:

- *Implementation Costs*: The initial implementation costs can be a barrier, especially for small and medium-sized organizations. Developing the IT infrastructure, purchasing software licenses, training users, and integrating with existing systems require considerable investments. The cost of RPA solutions depends on multiple parameters and can vary greatly depending on the level and complexity of automation and the solution vendor's pricing. Generally, a single bot costs from $5,000 to $15,000+, and the automation of several processes can be valued at up to $300,000. However, the cost-benefit analysis shows that these investments pay off in the medium term by increasing efficiency and reducing errors.
- *Technical Skills*: Moving from traditional workplace setups to a digital environment with RPA requires some consideration. RPA is far quicker to implement than many new software tools. However, that is not to say there are no growing pains. Indeed, transformation must be carefully planned with requirements and potential steps. Acceptance of new

technologies requires a process of cultural adaptation, effective communication, and continuous staff training.

- *Resistance to Change*: In spite of the benefits of RPA for HR staff, it is common for employees to oppose its implementation due to concerns on their part, such as job displacement or salary cuts. Leaders should use a human-centric change management approach that takes into account employee concerns and fears. When new employees do not feel some sort of emotional tie to the company within the first few months on the job, they tend not to be engaged.
- *Regulatory Compliance:* Regulations are in a constant state of flux, leaving HR teams struggling to keep up. HR managers have to comply with complex and ever-changing regulations when it comes to reporting, which is strictly required by labor law. Often, HR departments are responsible for ensuring compliance with various regulations. With consistent and accurate data handling, RPA software can help highly regulated HR departments comply with regulations. RPA can automatically track and monitor changes in labor laws, generate compliance reports, and notify relevant stakeholders about necessary actions.

10.7 Future Of Robotic Process Automation In Human Resources

As RPA technology continues to develop, the demand for workers with the ability to work alongside and manage the technology will increase. This means that workers who are not able to adapt and learn these new skills will be left behind in the job market.

Many jobs, as well as the human skills needed for those jobs, will change over time, but will not be eliminated. New digital skills will be needed so that HR can understand the power and capabilities associated with RPA technology and continually seek out areas for deployment. RPA implementation will require organizations to redesign roles and workflows [16]. In the future, automation will be used to make decisions on hiring the right people since RPA tools can also make decisions and recommendations free from human bias.

10.8 Conclusion

Robotic process automation is transforming HR operations by automating mundane tasks and enabling HR professionals to focus on strategic endeavors. Over the years, RPA has evolved from automating basic administrative tasks to supporting more complex functions, such as recruitment, onboarding, employee engagement, and retention strategies. The adoption of robotic process automation (RPA) in human resources has proven to be a game-changer, streamlining repetitive administrative tasks and improving efficiency across various HR functions, from recruitment to retention.

Understanding the evolution and impact of RPA in HR is crucial for organizations looking to leverage automation for greater operational efficiency while maintaining a positive employee experience. While RPA can automate administrative processes, it cannot replace the human element required for building strong employee relationships and fostering a positive organizational culture. As the cost of purchasing RPA technology begins to drop, more HR leaders will consider using it. More information about robotic process automation in human resources can be found in the books [17,18].

References

[1] "How robotic process automation (RPA) is optimizing 'business-as-usual'" August 2021, https://medium.com/elucidate-ai/how-robotic-process-automation-rpa-is-optimizing-business-as-usual-1c5e5c46ef43

[2] K. Aleksandrovich, "RPA in human resources: 10 use cases, examples & best tools," September 2024,

https://www.itransition.com/rpa/hr

[3] M. N. O. Sadiku, S. A. Ajayi, and J. O. Sadiku, "Robotic process automation in human resources," *International Journal of Trend in Scientific Research and Development,* vol. 10, no. 1, January-February, 2026, pp. 713-720.

[4] N. Komitsky, "Putting robotic process automation to work in the federal government,"

https://www.managementconcepts.com/resource/putting-robotic-process-automation-to-work-in-the-federal-government/

[5] "What is robotic process automation (RPA)? How does it work?" February 2023,

https://solidpro-es.com/what-is-robotic-process-automation-rpa-how-it-works/

[6] F. Caltin, "RPA in finance," February 2020,

https://www.plutushealthinc.com/post/rpa-in-finance

[7] "Absolutely everything you need to know about robotic process automation,"

https://www.blueprism.com/guides/robotic-process-automation-rpa/

[8] S. Donnelly, "5 Benefits of robotic process automation in finance," September 2022,

https://www.financealliance.io/5-benefits-of-robotic-process-automation-in-finance/

[9] "Robotic process automation in finance," September 2023,

https://kmbs.konicaminolta.us/blog/robotic-process-automation-in-finance/

[10] "Robotic process automation in finance,"

https://planergy.com/blog/robotic-process-automation-finance/

https://www.uipath.com/resources/automation-whitepapers/robotic-process-automation-in-telecommunications-csps

[11] V. Sharma, "The evolution of robotic process automation in human resources: From recruitment to retention," *International Journal of Multidisciplinary Research and Growth Evaluation,* vol. 5, no. 5, September-October 2024, pp. 1053-1057.

[12] P. K. Laxmipuram, "Streamlining HR processes: An in-depth analysis of robotic process automation (RPA) integration," *International Journal of Computer Trends and Technology*, vol. 72, no.1, January 2024, pp. 68-71.

[13] "Top 8 use cases of robotic process automation in HR," https://automationedge.com/blogs/top-8-rpa-use-cases-in-hr/

[14] "Simplify your human resource operations using robotic process automation (RPA)," August 2024,

https://www.linkedin.com/pulse/simplify-your-human-resource-operations-using-robotic-zesec

[15] "Robotic process automation (RPA) in HR: Case studies, examples, benefits & challenges in human resources,"

https://www.zaptest.com/robotic-process-automation-rpa-in-hr-case-studies-examples-benefits-challenges-in-human-resources

[16] G. Lawton, "What does robotic process automation mean for HR operations?" December 2021,

https://www.techtarget.com/searchhrsoftware/tip/What-does-robotic-process-automation-mean-for-HR-operations

[17] P. M. McCaulay, *Conquer Robotics and Automation Technician Careers: Guide to Jobs in Electrical and Instrumentation, Process Control and Automation, Programmable ... Industrial Automation (Vocational Guidance).* Independently Published, 2025.

[18] S. Strohmeier (ed.), *Handbook of Research on Artificial Intelligence in Human Resource Management.* Edward Elgar Publishing, 2022.

CHAPTER 11 ROBOTIC PROCESS AUTOMATION IN CUSTOMER SERVICE

"We hold these truths to be self-evident: that all men are created equal; that they are endowed by their Creator with certain unalienable rights; that among these are life, liberty, and the pursuit of happiness."
Thomas Jefferson.

11.1 Introduction

Robotic process automation (RPA) utilizes automated software, software robots, or "bots" to automate repetitive and rule-based tasks that human agents previously performed. These bots can be programmed to handle a wide range of activities, including data entry, form processing, order fulfillment, information retrieval, or even complex decision-making processes. Think of RPA bots as digital workers that log into applications, copy data, fill forms, and follow if-then rules, all without human intervention. RPA tools and bots interact with applications and systems just like humans, following predefined rules and instructions. RPA mainly focuses on automating manual, routine tasks, such as data entry, form filling, and screen scraping. By automating manual processes and augmenting human efforts, RPA implementations have paved the way for enhanced operational efficiency and improved customer experiences.

Robotic process automation involves creating software "robots" that interact with computer systems in a human-like manner. This includes opening websites, clicking links, downloading files, moving or extracting data, and much more. By integrating RPA into customer service (CS) workflows, businesses can enhance efficiency and allocate human agents to more complex issues, improving overall customer satisfaction while automating customer experiences. Figure 11.1 provides a definition of robotic process automation [1], while Figure 11.2 shows some customer service professionals [2].

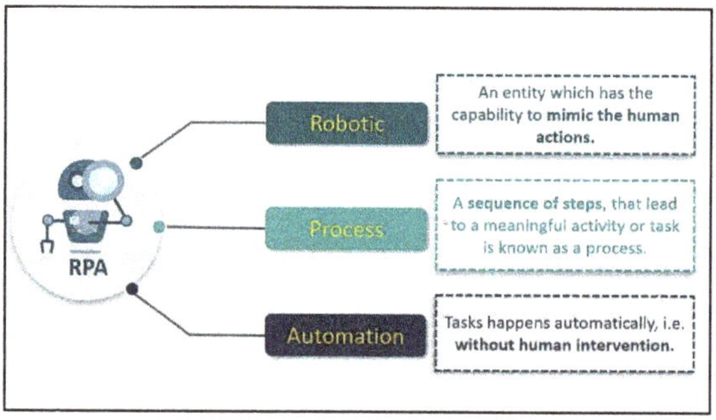

Figure 11.1 A definition of robotic process automation [1].

Figure 11.2 Some customer service professionals [2].

Robotic process automation (RPA) technology uses software robots or bots to automate repetitive, rule-based tasks that humans typically perform. This innovative technology is reshaping customer experiences across various industries. It is a breakthrough technology that is revolutionizing customer service by automating repetitive tasks, streamlining workflows, and enhancing overall efficiency. By leveraging RPA, companies can automate tedious tasks, leading to increased efficiency and cost savings. As a result, employees can spend more time on tasks like innovating, being creative, connecting with customers, and building relationships. By implementing RPA, organizations achieve greater operational efficiency, strengthen customer engagement, and maintain a competitive edge [3].

This chapter explores the transformative impact of robotic process automation on customer service and support teams. It begins with explaining the concept of robotic process automation (RPA). It describes RPA in customer service and provides some of its applications. It highlights the benefits and challenges of RPA in customer service. It predicts the future of RPA in customer service. The last section concludes with comments.

11.2 What Is Robotic Process Automation?

Among the various forms of artificial intelligence, RPA stands out for its potential to significantly increase workforce productivity by reducing or eliminating the need to do repetitive tasks manually.

Popular applications of RPA include data entry, data reconciliation, spreadsheet manipulation, systems integration, automated data reporting, analytics, email notifications, acquisitions, administrative services, finance, human resources, mission assurance, strategic communications, travel reimbursements, claims processing, and customer outreach and communications. These are just a few examples of the ways RPA is being used to remove the burden of manual, repetitive, and duplicative tasks from public service workers [4].

Robotic process automation is a form of automation software. It is a technology that can automate repetitive, rules-based tasks. Like an Excel macro operating within a spreadsheet, RPA can record actions performed across a personal computer, access systems, and perform specific tasks for human users. It uses software robots, more commonly called "bots," that mimic basic human-computer interactions. Figure 11.3 shows the symbol of RPA [5], while Figure 11.4 shows processes that RPA can automate [6]. Most industries use RPA. The government does too. Due to the repetitive nature of some tasks, the probability of human error increases. One way to eliminate errors is by using RPA. Robotic process automation solutions fall into three key categories: attended RPA, unattended RPA, and hybrid RPA, as shown in Figure 11.5 [7].

Figure 11.3 Symbol of RPA [5].

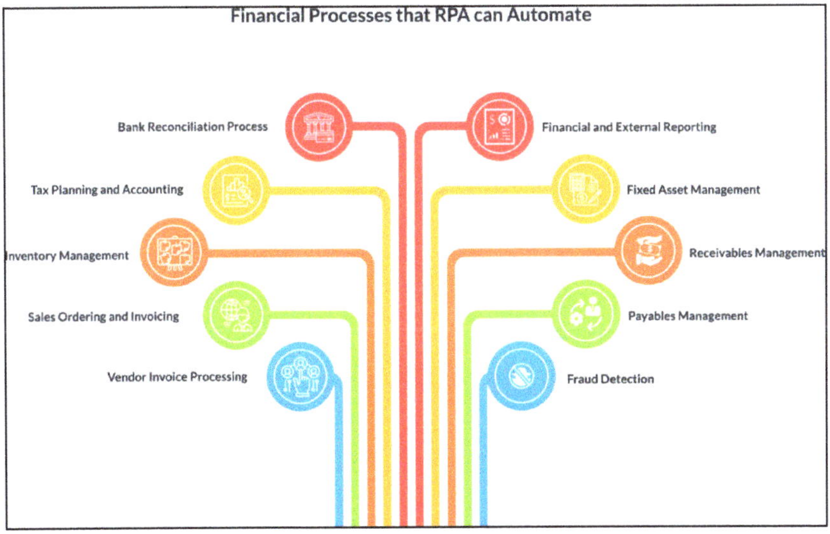

Figure 11.4 Processes that RPA can automate [6].

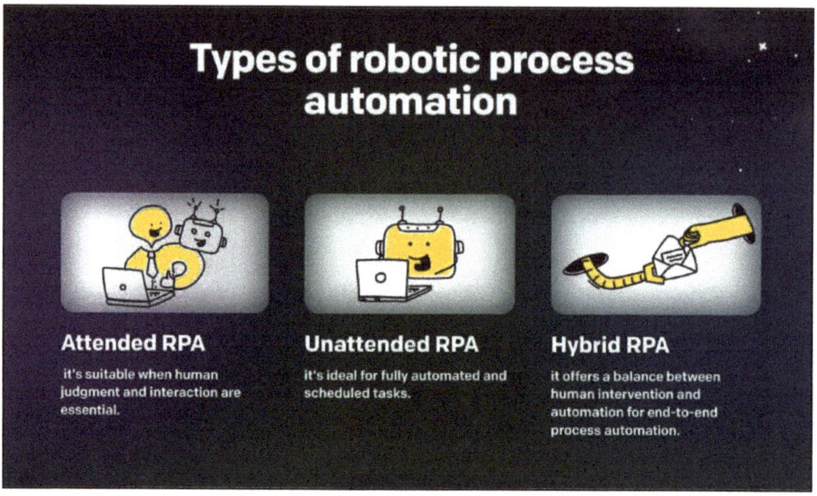

Figure 11.5 Three types of RPA [7].

Robotic process automation is a type of software that mimics the activity of a human being in carrying out a task within a process. It is a technology that automates repetitive tasks using software robots. RPA uses a set of automation tools to automate repetitive tasks and manual processes performed electronically. Since RPA can automate tasks that are rule-based, manual, repetitive, and tedious, delivering the highest levels of accuracy and eradicating human errors, it is a seamless fit for the finance industry. Here are some specific examples of what RPA in finance can do [8]:

- Opening emails and joining attachments
- Automatically logging into various applications on the web
- Shifting folders and files
- Copying and pasting

- Completing forms
- Collecting data from databases and the web
- Making calculations
- Connecting to system API
- Extracting structured data from documents
- Gathering stats from social media
- Following if/then decisions and rules

Some of these tasks are displayed in Figure 11.6 [7].

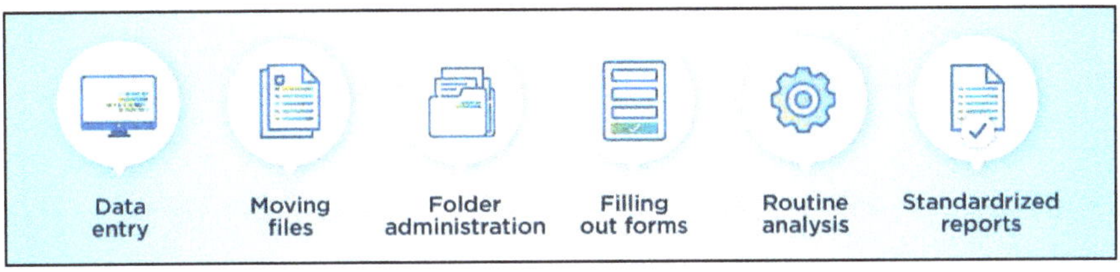

Figure 11.6 Some tasks RPA can perform [7].

At its core, robotic process automation (RPA) is a tool designed to mimic rule-based business processes, performing them seamlessly and without fatigue. RPA is a rule-driven method that is limited in its application. The technology functions much like a Microsoft Excel macro; the key difference is in power and reach. It follows set rules, similar to how an Excel macro works, to do things like move files or log into accounts. Growing as a popular solution in finance and accounting, RPA refers to software technology or "software robots" with artificial intelligence (AI) and machine learning (ML) capabilities. The "software robots" have the ability to learn and complete a high

volume of rules-based, repetitive tasks and business processes. They have the capacity to operate much faster than humans, with 100% precision and reliability, working around the clock.

Finance and human resources are just two examples of departments likely to have many use cases that RPA can help solve. Some examples of good use cases for RPA in finance include processing customer orders, ensuring timely vendor payments, and managing period-end financial close processes. For human resources, some examples include employee onboarding, time tracking, and leave of absence management. Processes where human judgment is needed are not appropriate for RPA since RPA automations rely on clear, consistently applied rules [9].

Along with RPA, one should be aware of both business process automation (BPA) and digital process automation (DPA) – two commonly used automation technologies that robotics process automation can be paired with to optimize and streamline a digital transformation. BPA refers to the use of technology to automate complex, multi-step workflows, typically very specific to a company's core business functions. DPA offers dual power by automating processes from end to end and optimizing common workflows that involve external human interactions (i.e., sales, management). Separately, RPA and AI are quite powerful, but leveraging them together is undoubtedly advantageous to any financial institution. When deployed together, AI is the "brains" behind RPA's bots [10].

11.3 Robotic Process Automation In Customer Service

Traditionally, customer service has relied heavily on human agents to handle queries, resolve issues, and provide assistance. However, this manual approach often resulted in delays, inconsistencies, and human errors, leading to customer dissatisfaction and increased business costs. Traditional customer service methods, known for long wait times and frustrating phone menus, fail to keep up. The advent of robotic process automation (RPA) has revolutionized customer care, empowering businesses with intelligent process automation capabilities. RPA technology has emerged as a catalyst, seamlessly integrating with existing systems and streamlining recurring tasks. By automating repetitive tasks and ensuring efficient and error-free results, RPA streamlines operations and enhances the customer experience. By taking over mundane tasks, RPA allows customer support agents to focus on more complex and value-added activities, such as solving intricate issues, providing personalized assistance, or nurturing customer relationships. With RPA, customers can experience quicker resolutions, improved accuracy, and round-the-clock support, enhancing overall satisfaction and loyalty [7].

In customer service, robotic process automation (RPA) refers to using software bots to automate repetitive tasks like data entry, ticket routing, and order processing. These bots mimic human actions to streamline processes, reducing errors and response times. The RPA technology expedites responses and boosts accuracy, thereby elevating customer satisfaction levels. Unlike traditional software requiring deep API integration, RPA operates at the user interface level.

11.4 Applications Of Robotic Process Automation In Customer Service

From handling routine inquiries and processing requests to accelerating response times and improving data accuracy, RPA has emerged as a game-changer, allowing organizations to deliver seamless and efficient support services. Common examples of how you can utilize RPA in your customer care include the following [7,11,12]:

- *Automation:* As shown in Figure 11.7, RPA has the potential to automate up to 80% of customer interactions [11]. RPA bots can be configured to analyze incoming customer emails, extract relevant information, and generate automated responses for common inquiries. RPA can automate updating customer information or entering data into CRM or ticketing systems. RPA enables self-service options for customers by automating responses to frequently asked questions. RPA can automate order processing tasks, such as order entry, payment verification, and tracking updates. Manually creating new customer accounts is time-intensive, requiring data entry across multiple systems. RPA can automate the busywork while ensuring accurate onboarding. Automation Anywhere is a well-known RPA software that offers comprehensive solutions for customer care automation. It provides a range of features such as data entry, ticket management, content generation, and integration with CRM systems.

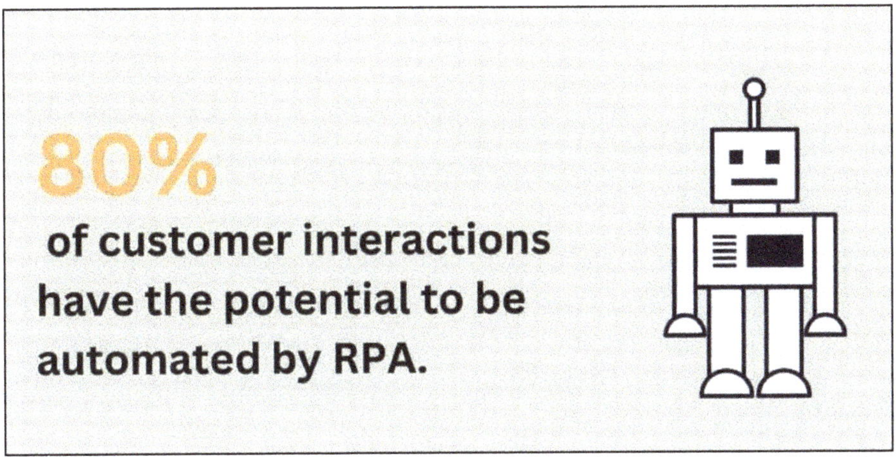

Figure 11.7 RPA has the potential to automate up to 80% of customer interactions [11].

- *Report Generation:* RPA tools can collect and consolidate data from multiple sources to generate reports on key customer support metrics, such as response times, ticket volumes, customer satisfaction scores, and agent performance. These reports can help identify trends, optimize processes, and make data-driven decisions. RPA-powered customer service bots make use of NLP and OCR to decipher customer complaints received via emails or text messages. They extract complaint data, input it into spreadsheets and text documents, and generate reports.
- *Data Governance:* Customer service processes generate a vast amount of data, including customer interactions, inquiries, and resolutions. Managing this data efficiently within RPA systems can be challenging, especially when dealing with diverse data formats and sources. RPA is centered around tasks that nurture customer relationships. It allows employees to concentrate on tasks that have a direct impact on customer

relationships. It supports customer agents by automating repetitive tasks, freeing up their time to develop their skills and enhance customer interactions. RPA bots for customer service can retrieve data from the ticket database and handle basic client inquiries.

- *Data Analysis:* Extracting actionable insights from customer data is essential for enhancing service quality, personalization, and decision-making. However, analyzing large volumes of unstructured or semi-structured data manually can be time-consuming and prone to errors. Improved data analytics is a significant benefit offered by RPA. For example, utilizing RPA to gather and categorize data into predefined formats enables businesses to streamline decision-making processes. It also allows them to allocate resources more effectively across different levels of their organizations.
- *Data Entry:* A customer support agent frequently needs to upload new information into the system or open a new ticket to fix the client's issue. They must go through a variety of programs to do this. Each step adds to the process's sluggishness and makes it more prone to mistakes since agents must input data manually. RPA offers auto-fill and similar functionalities. These capabilities significantly decrease the need for human interaction while also eliminating the possibility of inaccuracy.
- *Chatbots:* Chatbots serve as the first line of assistance and are accessible 24/7. A significant advantage of adopting RPA-based chatbots is their continuous, all-around availability – ready to be utilized to manage customer support 24 hours a day, seven days a week. Unlike humans, chatbots do not use time as a parameter. Consequently, using chatbots to answer

after-hours inquiries frequently proves feasible and cost-effective

- *Sentiment Analysis:* AI analyzes voice sentiment through tone, pitch, and stress indicators. For text channels, it evaluates emotions like anger or confusion. When sentiment drops, RPA instantly routes alerts to supervisors, displays recommendations to agents, and triggers escalation to specialized teams. Make informed choices backed by accurate customer sentiment analysis, which will lead to better experiences and increased satisfaction.

11.5 Benefits

RPA brings efficiency, accuracy, and scalability to business processes by automating repetitive tasks, reducing errors, and freeing up human workers to focus on higher-value activities. It empowers organizations to deliver faster, more accurate, and more personalized customer service, leading to increased customer satisfaction, loyalty, and retention. RPA assists representatives by retrieving relevant information, reducing their workload, and enabling them to focus on complex issues. Other benefits include the following [7,11,13]:

- *Cost Reduction:* One of the primary reasons for adopting RPA is its potential for significant cost reduction. By automating time-intensive, repetitive tasks, companies can reallocate human resources more strategically, reducing the reliance on manual labor and lowering operational expenses.
  RPA minimizes manual intervention, reducing labor costs and operational inefficiencies. By automating repetitive tasks like data entry and query resolution, you achieve

significant savings, allowing resources to be allocated more effectively.

- *24/7 Availability:* With RPA handling routine tasks, your customer service can operate round the clock, providing support anytime. RPA enables round-the-clock support, ensuring assistance whenever customers need it. Automated processes alleviate the burden on your customer service staff, allowing them to focus on high-value tasks. Customers can access help whenever needed through self-service options, which leads to higher customer satisfaction.
- *Enhanced Accuracy:* Human errors not only extend the duration of processes but also shape customers' perceptions of an organization as less competent and dependable than it is. One of the most significant advantages of RPA lies in its ability to reduce human errors through task automation, providing immense relief to employees who no longer need to spend hours rectifying mistakes. RPA optimizes tasks, mitigating human errors. RPA is highly effective at performing structured tasks with exceptional accuracy, ensuring processes are standardized, and customer interactions remain consistent.
- *Enhanced Processes:* RPA enhances business processes, maintains compliance, reduces errors, and increases efficiency by leveraging customer service. Basically, it may ensure that all changes to your system are smoothly recorded. Besides RPA, customer service robots run inspections and update your workflows in the background.
- *Operational Efficiency:* One of the primary benefits of implementing RPA in customer care is its ability to enhance operational efficiency. By automating routine tasks,

organizations can significantly reduce response times, minimize errors, and simultaneously handle a higher volume of customer inquiries. RPA promises immense service productivity gains through around-the-clock automation of repetitive processes.

- *Customer Experience:* A strong customer experience is essential in today's market. Providing prompt, accurate, and personalized support is crucial for customer satisfaction. However, customer service agents spend countless hours on repetitive manual tasks like copying data between systems, filing paperwork, and answering routine questions. This frustrates customers with long waits and distracts agents from higher-value work. It also leads to errors when agents have to rush through repetitive chores instead of focusing on service quality. RPA tools streamline interactions, making them faster, more personalized, and more efficient, improving satisfaction and reducing support costs.
- *Scalability:* RPA brings scalability and flexibility to customer support operations. RPA's scalability offers a compelling advantage, empowering organizations to manage fluctuating customer demands without expanding their physical workforce. As businesses grow and customer demands increase, RPA can easily adapt and handle higher workloads without additional hiring or training. The bots can be scaled up or down based on the fluctuating demand, ensuring consistent support and preventing bottlenecks during peak periods.
- *Personalization:* Integrating RPA with other advanced technologies allows businesses to deliver highly personalized customer experiences. By accessing and processing data from various sources in real-time, RPA supports customized responses that meet individual customer needs more

effectively. The seamless integration elevates the overall service quality and deepens customer relationships through personalized, data-informed interactions that resonate more strongly.

11.6 Challenges

While RPA offers numerous benefits, balancing automation and human intervention is essential. While bots can handle repetitive tasks effectively, they may lack the corresponding empathy, intuition, and problem-solving skills that human agents possess. RPA is designed to mimic human actions and does not possess cognitive abilities. Other challenges include the following [11,14,15]:

- *Resistance to Change*: Despite the benefits, many customers still prefer human representatives. They favor live service agents over bots and claim that human touch is very important. To shift perceptions, setting proper expectations through customer education will be crucial. Companies must carefully design workflows to smoothly transfer customers from bots to human agents when needed.
- *Limitations:* While great for repetitive tasks, RPA bots rely on programmed rules and lack the flexibility to handle novel situations. No technology is a "silver bullet" that solves every problem or works flawlessly in 100% of situations. It is important to keep in mind that there are limitations to RPA tools.
- *Modulating Needs:* Customer service demands can fluctuate significantly based on factors such as seasonality, promotional events, or market trends. Scaling RPA processes to

accommodate varying workload volumes while maintaining performance levels can be a challenge. RPA programs efficiently execute various customer-driven tasks in minimal time and with fewer errors compared to human employees. Moreover, RPA enables faster transactions and resolutions.

- *Complexity:* Today's CS teams have more tools than ever, but that is not always good. A complex technical environment for customer service teams can lead to slowdowns, errors, and other difficulties. As companies grow and scale up, processes that once seemed simple can become increasingly complex. Without efforts to grow those workflows to suit new levels of need, bottlenecks and poor results are often the outcome. The most common challenge, a steady volume of support requests, can overwhelm even dedicated teams.

11.7 Future Of Robotic Process Automation In Customer Service

As businesses continue to embrace the power of RPA, it is evident that this transformative technology will remain at the forefront of customer support, driving innovation and propelling businesses toward a more efficient and customer-centric future. The continuous advancement of RPA technology points to promising, more sophisticated applications in the near future. With innovations in artificial intelligence and machine learning, RPA is becoming increasingly intuitive and adaptive. This progress implies that future implementations will excel in understanding context, anticipating customer needs, and making autonomous decisions aligned with business strategies. As RPA becomes more advanced, businesses are reimagining traditional service approaches to deliver superior, real-time solutions that cater to evolving customer needs. This progression highlights RPA's critical role in modernizing business operations and maintaining a competitive edge [13].

11.8 Conclusion

Robotic process automation (RPA) is a software technology that deploys and manages software robots that mimic human actions when interacting with digital systems and software. It is revolutionizing customer service by introducing software robots capable of handling repetitive tasks with unprecedented efficiency and accuracy. It is fundamentally changing customer interactions by automating repetitive, rule-based tasks that were once handled by human agents. It improves customer service by reducing administrative and back-office workload. It reduces the time spent on routine operations and minimizes the risk of human error, freeing teams to focus on strategic, high-value work.

The adoption of robotic process automation is accelerating across the industry. It has evolved from a back-office tool to a critical contact center component. Organizations embracing RPA understand what it really is, choose the right processes to automate, and view intelligent automation as strategic enablement. RPA tools will play a critical role in redefining how companies approach customer service. More information about robotic process automation in customer service can be found in the books [16,17].

References

[1] "How robotic process automation (RPA) is optimizing 'business-as-usual'" August 2021, https://medium.com/elucidate-ai/how-robotic-process-automation-rpa-is-optimizing-business-as-usual-1c5e5c46ef43

[2] https://images.search.yahoo.com/search/images?p=images+of+customer+service+team&fr=mcafee&type=E210US1357G0&imgurl=https%3A%2F%2Fwww.outsource-consultants.com%2Fwp-content%2Fuploads%2F2020%2F10%2Fimg-inbound-call-center-services-customer-service.jpg#id=14&iurl=https%3A%2F%2Fwww.outsource-consultants.com%2Fwp-content%2Fuploads%2F2020%2F10%2Fimg-inbound-call-center-services-customer-service.jpg&action=click

[3] M. N. O. Sadiku and J. O. Sadiku, "Robotic process automation in customer service," *International Journal of Trend in Research and Development*, vol. 13, no. 1, January-February 2026, pp. 125-129.

[4] N. Komitsky, "Putting robotic process automation to work in the federal government,"

https://www.managementconcepts.com/resource/putting-robotic-process-automation-to-work-in-the-federal-government/

[5] "What is robotic process automation (RPA)? How does it work?" February 2023,

https://solidpro-es.com/what-is-robotic-process-automation-rpa-how-it-works/

[6] F. Caltin, "RPA in finance," February 2020,

https://www.plutushealthinc.com/post/rpa-in-finance

[7] W. Masternak, "A closer look at robotic process automation in customer support,"

https://www.helpdesk.com/learn/robotic-process-automation/

[8] S. Donnelly, "5 Benefits of robotic process automation in finance," September 2022,

https://www.financealliance.io/5-benefits-of-robotic-process-automation-in-finance/

[9] "Robotic process automation in finance," September 2023,

https://kmbs.konicaminolta.us/blog/robotic-process-automation-in-finance/

[10] "Robotic process automation in finance,"

https://planergy.com/blog/robotic-process-automation-finance/

https://www.uipath.com/resources/automation-whitepapers/robotic-process-automation-in-telecommunications-csps

[11] "How does robotic process automation in customer service work?"

https://saufter.io/robotic-process-automation-customer-service/

[12] "10 Use cases for RPA in the contact center,"

https://www.cxtoday.com/contact-center/10-uses-cases-for-rpa-in-the-contact-center/

[13] V. Miller, "Reimagining customer service: The rise of RPA technology," December 2024,

https://techbullion.com/reimagining-customer-service-the-rise-of-rpa-technology/

[14] P. Christiano, "Top 7 RPA use cases to transform customer service in 2025," November 2023,

https://expertbeacon.com/rpa-customer-service/#google_vignette

[15] "Enhancing customer service outcomes with AI and robotic process automation (RPA)," July 2023,

https://www.tungstenautomation.com/learn/blog/enhancing-customer-service-outcomes-with-ai-and-robotic-process-automation

[16] D. De, J. S. Banerjee, and S. Bhattacharyya (eds.), *Confluence of Artificial Intelligence and Robotic Process Automation*. Springer, 2023.

[17] C. Czarnecki and P. Fettke (eds.), *Robotic Process Automation: Management, Technology, Applications.* De Gruyter, 2021.

CHAPTER 12
ROBOTIC PROCESS AUTOMATION IN GOVERNMENT

"My fellow Americans: ask not what your country can do for you—ask what you can do for your country."
John F. Kennedy

12.1 Introduction

It is difficult to overstate the role technology plays in the way governments operate. Governments have learned the hard way that it is next to impossible to operate in the 21st century without technology. With electronic permitting laws being passed in states like New Jersey and Florida back in 2021, the writing is on the wall that local governments will be going through a digital revolution in the coming years [1]. A component of the revolution is the robotic process automation (RPA). There is a transition trend toward "digital government" and consideration for new technologies adoption at scale, including RPA.

Robotic process automation (RPA) uses software tools driven by rules to automate predictable routines and tasks through coordinated actions that mimic human behavior. RPA employs software bots that mimic human actions to interact with existing applications, systems, and data sources. These bots are designed to perform simple, time-consuming, and rules-based tasks such as data entry, form filling, document processing, and report generation. Just like people, these robots are able to leverage a computer screen, keyboards, online systems, and data to get work done for a government entity without the labor cost or risk of human error. With RPA handling simple but time-consuming tasks, municipal workers can spend their time on more important work.

Robotic process automation (RPA) is the process of using robotic software technology to automate digital tasks and replace manual processes with digital best practices. It includes any software tool or utility that replaces repetitive, labor-intensive tasks with an automated process. It is a relatively new software technology used for automating high-volume and mundane business processes. RPA is transforming government operations by streamlining time-consuming tasks and improving service delivery. It is used in the government sector for several reasons, including its ability to automate mundane and repetitive tasks, reduce costs, and free up human labor for more strategic duties. Examples abound of the technology being used at the global, federal, state, and local levels [2].

The purpose of this chapter is to explain the adoption of robotic process automation (RPA) in the government sector. It begins with describing robotic process automation.

It discusses robotic process automation in government and provides some of its applications. It highlights some of the benefits and challenges of robotic process automation in government. The last section concludes with comments.

12.2 What Is Robotic Process Automation?

Among the various forms of artificial intelligence, RPA stands out for its potential to significantly increase workforce productivity by reducing or eliminating the need to do repetitive tasks manually. Popular applications of RPA include data entry, data reconciliation, spreadsheet manipulation, systems integration, automated data reporting, analytics, email notifications, acquisitions, administrative services, finance, human resources, mission assurance, strategic communications, travel reimbursements, claims processing, and customer outreach and communications. These are just a few examples of the ways RPA is being used to remove the burden of manual, repetitive, and duplicative tasks from public service workers [3].

Robotic process automation is a form of automation software. It is a technology that can automate repetitive, rules-based tasks. Like an Excel macro operating within a spreadsheet, RPA can record actions performed across a personal computer, access systems, and perform specific tasks for human users. It uses software robots, more commonly called "bots," that mimic basic human-computer interactions. Figure 12.1 shows the symbol of RPA [4], while Figure 12.2 shows processes that RPA can automate [5]. Most industries use RPA. The government does too. Due to the repetitive nature of some tasks, the probability of human error increases. One way to eliminate errors is by using RPA. Robotic process automation solutions fall into three key categories: attended RPA, unattended RPA, and hybrid RPA, as shown in Figure 12.3 [6].

Figure 12.1 Symbol of RPA [4].

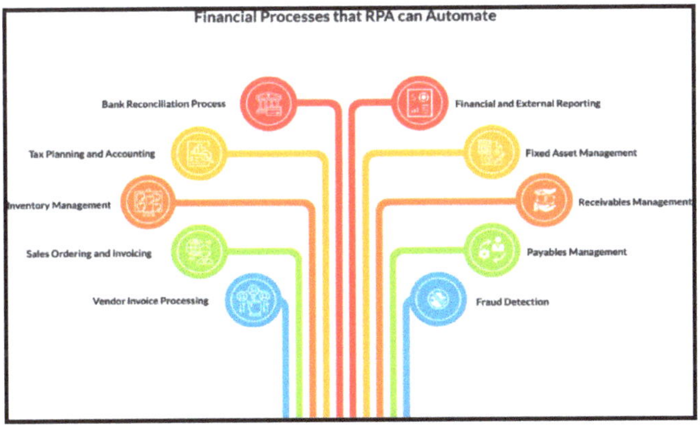

Figure 12.2 Processes that RPA can automate [5].

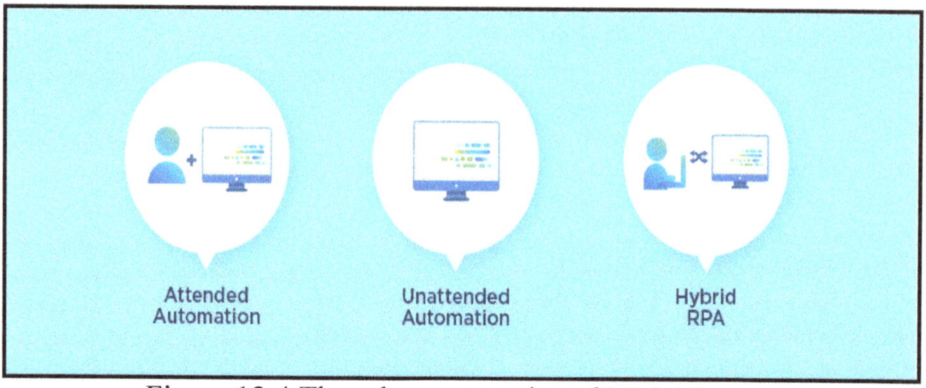

Figure 12.4 Three key categories of RPA [6].

Robotic process automation is a type of software that mimics the activity of a human being in carrying out a task within a process. It is a technology that automates repetitive tasks using software robots. RPA uses a set of automation tools to automate repetitive tasks and manual processes performed electronically. Since RPA can automate tasks that are rule-based, manual, repetitive, and tedious, delivering the highest levels of accuracy and eradicating human errors, it is a seamless fit for the finance industry. Here are some specific examples of what RPA in finance can do [7]:

- Opening emails and joining attachments
- Automatically logging into various applications on the web
- Shifting folders and files
- Copying and pasting
- Completing forms
- Collecting data from databases and the web
- Making calculations

- Connecting to system API
- Extracting structured data from documents
- Gathering stats from social media
- Following if/then decisions and rules

Some of these tasks are displayed in Figure 12.4 [6].

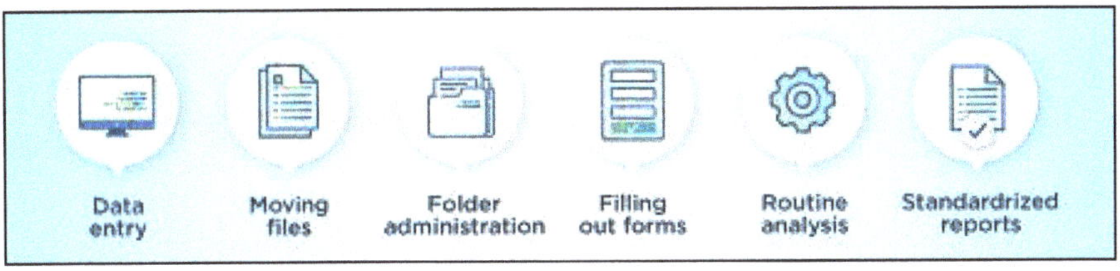

Figure 12.4 Some tasks RPA can perform [6].

At its core, robotic process automation (RPA) is a tool designed to mimic rule-based business processes, performing them seamlessly and without fatigue. RPA is a rule-driven method that is limited in its application. The technology functions much like a Microsoft Excel macro; the key difference is in power and reach. It follows set rules, similar to how an Excel macro works, to do things like move files or log into accounts. Growing as a popular solution in finance and accounting, RPA refers to software technology or "software robots" with artificial intelligence (AI) and machine learning (ML) capabilities. The "software robots" have the ability to learn and complete a high volume of rules-based, repetitive tasks and business processes. They have the capacity to operate much faster than humans, with 100% precision and reliability, working around the clock.

Finance and human resources are just two examples of departments likely to have many use cases that RPA can help solve. Some examples of good use cases for RPA in finance include processing customer orders, ensuring timely vendor payments, and managing period-end financial close processes. For human resources, some examples include employee onboarding, time tracking, and leave of absence management. Processes where human judgment is needed are not appropriate for RPA since RPA automations rely on clear, consistently applied rules [8].

Along with RPA, one should be aware of both business process automation (BPA) and digital process automation (DPA) – two commonly used automation technologies that robotics process automation can be paired with to optimize and streamline a digital transformation. BPA refers to the use of technology to automate complex, multi-step workflows, typically very specific to a company's core business functions. DPA offers dual power by automating processes from end to end and optimizing common workflows that involve external human interactions (i.e., sales, management). Separately, RPA and AI are quite powerful, but leveraging them together is undoubtedly advantageous to any financial institution. When deployed together, AI is the "brains" behind RPA's bots [9].

12.3 Robotic Process Automation In Government

Robotic process automation (RPA) in government uses software "robots" to automate repetitive, rules-based tasks, improving efficiency, accuracy, and speed in citizen services, data processing, and administrative functions like permit processing, tax filing, and procurement. The federal government and other public agencies have adopted RPA to streamline operations, though agencies must also address risks related to data security and the proper management of automated processes. For governments struggling to recruit new public workers, these systems can replace certain administrative roles, thereby saving money for government budgets and allocating more funds to improve constituent services. These tasks are related to clerical work and data-entry for businesses and government agencies, or perform tasks that are tedious and time-consuming to save manpower and resources for municipal workers.

RPA has already demonstrated its ability to reduce costs and increase efficiency in multiple industries, prompting officials from governments and the public sector to consider it as a potential solution for enhancing citizen services. RPA is increasingly becoming popular as a way to speed up government work. Work related to administrative data-entry and reporting roles that previously required hours to complete can now be done by robot software in significantly shorter periods of time.

12.4 Applications Of Robotic Process Automation In Government

Robotic process automation (RPA) is software that is designed to accomplish simple tasks that formerly needed to be done by the human workforce. RPA is being put to work in a widening range of applications, including efforts to streamline data collection and processing, document management, identity verification, and to respond automatically to citizens' information requests. With the ability to automate tasks with RPAs, governments can address understaffed, overworked departments, spend less time recruiting government workers, and eliminate inefficient manual processes. Common application areas include [1,10,11]:

- *Automation:* Governments have to deal with repetitive, labor-intensive tasks like document processing, information dissemination, data management, and security compliance. Manual data entry is prone to mistakes that can cause delays and dissatisfaction among applicants. Tax calculations often involve processing vast amounts of data, which can be both time-consuming and error-prone when done manually. RPA helps by automating data extraction, validation, and routing tasks, ensuring faster processing times. By automating this process, governments can save time otherwise spent on manual audits and assessments. This eliminates bottlenecks and reduces the burden on employees while improving the citizen experience. Processing tax refunds manually can be frustrating for citizens and time-intensive for employees. RPA reduces processing times by automatically verifying taxpayer information, matching it against records, and flagging potential discrepancies. RPA can be used to automate applications for and renewals of driver's licenses, passports, tax forms, and records about employment, healthcare, and insurance coverage.

- *License Registration:* Constituents and business-owners now wield the power to file for licenses online, at any time. License requests will be automatically accessible from the cloud, meaning municipal workers can approve or deny requests directly from the software application, no matter where they are working from. These include business registration, pet licenses, volunteer registration, and contract management.
- *Court House:* Your local courthouse has the potential to drastically reduce the amount of time spent on administrative tasks with court management software. When a constituent requests court records or court-hearing transcripts, robots can automatically send out the relevant documentation, saving a municipal worker time on the task.
- *Online Returns:* An RPA you likely interact with is online merchandise returns processing. When you start a return, the bot generates a message that confirms the return, issues a return receipt, adjusts the payment, and updates the merchant's inventory. Using RPA software allows workers to focus on more complex return processes or customer service issues.
- *Agentic Automation:* RPA has gone through several evolutions, first with intelligent automation (IA), then with artificial intelligence (AI), and next with enterprise AI. Now, we are in the next phase of automation: agentic automation, or agentic AI. In agentic process automation, AI agents can

complete more complex tasks with minimal human intervention. Simply give them a goal, and they will find the best way to achieve it.

- *Global Usage:* Examples of global uses of RPA abound. There are a number of federal agencies that are implementing RPA tools. The US federal government is pursuing robotic process automation technology to increase efficiency and effectiveness. The Navy has implemented RPA bots to capture screenshots of authorization letters for purchase orders. A city government in Japan has used RPA to reduce staff workload, improve service delivery to citizens, and resolve the challenges of new staff hiring and orientation. In the United Kingdom (UK), one of the largest government department agencies has automated routine tasks, increased efficiency, and improved decision-making. In Ireland, the Health Services Executive, which is the agency that provides all public health services to hospitals and communities throughout the country, has created their own RPA Centre of Excellence. Belgium is using RPA bots for job matching employment opportunities, focusing on workers' competencies instead of just professional experience or education.

12.5 Benefits

Robotic process automation (RPA) is transforming how government agencies operate, saving time, improving efficiency, and enhancing service delivery. It is an increasingly popular option for government agencies with legacy technology systems, complex workflows, and backlogs for approving applications for services. The government's program has improved with assistance from the software robots that can work without fatigue around the clock. RPA minimizes human errors that can occur during high-volume manual data processing. Other benefits include the following [12]:

- *Automation:* Automation is a smart, modern option to keep municipalities operating efficiently despite roadblocks or a lack of employee manpower. Automation programming has empowered humans to create a set of instructions to allow machines to mimic human knowledge extracted and learned from data sets and experiences. By automating mundane tasks, RPA frees up government employees for more complex work, reduces operational costs, and enhances overall citizen satisfaction. Automation reduces the need for extensive manual labor in repetitive tasks, leading to lower operational costs. Staff are freed from mundane, repetitive work to focus on more strategic, complex, and value-added activities. Robots can operate 24/7 without breaks, vacations, or sick days and can yield dramatic improvements in accuracy, cycle time, and productivity in transactional processes.
- *Minimizing Errors:* Manual processes often result in errors due to the volume of data being processed and human oversight. Payroll errors can lead to employee dissatisfaction and additional administrative tasks. RPA reduces errors by automatically verifying information and flagging inconsistencies. By minimizing errors and inefficiencies, governments avoid penalties and rework costs. This fosters trust between citizens and the government, as services are delivered more efficiently and reliably. Because there is no human involvement in the process, bots maintain the quality and accuracy of migrated data.

- *Cost Savings:* Lower operational costs are another outcome of using RPA for document handling and validation. RPA reduces operational costs by automating labor-intensive tasks, eliminating the need for extensive manual effort. Government agencies save resources by cutting down on paperwork, streamlining workflows, and reallocating staff to higher-priority areas. The cost-effectiveness of RPA not only optimizes budgets but also enhances service delivery without compromising quality.
- *Time Savings:* Bots can perform tasks with speed and precision, leading to faster service delivery and increased output. Whether we are dealing with payroll, updating records, or validating data, they can be completed with perfect accuracy using RPA in a third of the time it takes to process them manually. The effectiveness and productivity of governmental institutions can be increased by using bots in the workforce.
- *Legacy Systems:* RPA is particularly beneficial for governments with legacy technology systems, as it allows for automation without requiring significant system overhauls.
- *Building Trust:* With the accessibility to file paperwork online, and the reduced amount of time it will take for government workers to approve or deny applications, constituents will appreciate government innovations and have more trust in their local government officials.
- *Collaboration:* With relevant documentation, data, and records stored in the cloud, municipal workers across departments can access paperwork and collaborate with ease, eliminating traditional, unnecessary obstacles caused by paper-based processes and single-use software.

- *Customer Satisfaction:* Certain points in any customer experience journey will benefit from the "human touch." But for other areas, RPA technology offers many advantages for your customers. For example, RPA chatbots can also answer customer queries in real-time, 24/7. By taking care of laborious tasks, RPA gives your human customer service agents the time to manage more complex customer issues. They can focus on providing excellent personal responses for better customer satisfaction.

Some benefits of RPA are depicted in Figure 12.5 [6].

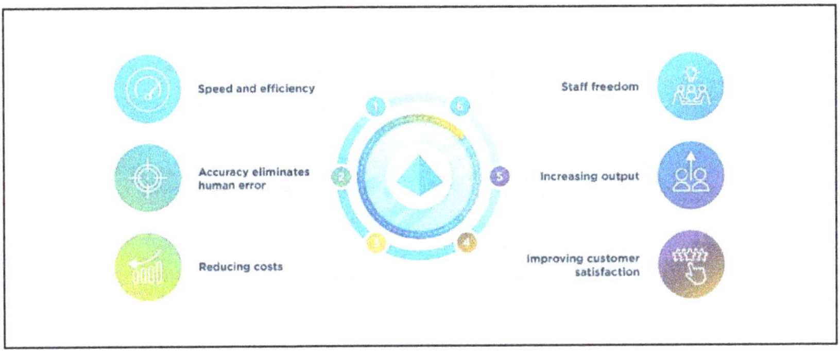

Figure 12.5 Some benefits of RPA [6].

12.6 Challenges

While one appreciates the benefits of RPA, the prospect of navigating from proof of concept to deployment can be quite intimidating. Adoption of RPA in the government and public sector faces several challenges. Among the key challenges are a lack of transparency in data processing and analysis, and inadequate privacy and security protections. Other challenges include the following [13,14]:

- *Bias:* In order for bots to operate effectively and be free from bias, they need to rely on information that is accurate and representative of the users being served. Anything that reduces the representativeness or completeness of the data introduces potential errors into the processing and must be avoided.
- *Transparency*: Having transparency in data processing and analysis is important. Both federal employees and the customers/clients being served must understand how bots operate and where they are drawing information. Being transparent about choices and processes aids the user experience and builds confidence in the applications.
- *Lack of Portability:* Automations built on a specific RPA platform are not always portable to other platforms. RPA tools can tightly couple agencies to a specific vendor. Vendor neutrality, support for different features, and rapid changes in pricing are to be expected.
- *Limited Ability:* RPA tools by themselves cannot dramatically improve the user experience of government services. Processes that are complex, require multiple steps, with multiple review and approval stages, often place an enormous administrative burden on those who use them. RPA is most effective when applied to well-defined processes with clear goals. Good candidates for RPA possess some or all of the following characteristics, they tend to be: static rules-based processes, requiring minimal human input or decision making; repetitive in nature; can be performed during off-peak hours; are data-driven and involve data manipulation; and have high error rates. Governance that includes process documentation

and audit trails for decisions made is essential to ensure bots are not performing unnecessary or redundant functions

- *Privacy:* There needs to be adequate privacy and security protections built into the applications. Having an RPA that respects the confidentiality of information and maintains the security of data compilation is of high priority. The RPA must operate within the standing privacy policies to ensure it maintains the privacy of personal information.
- *Job Losses:* Americans generally hold positive attitudes about technology innovation, although they worry about the impact on jobs and what automation will mean for future skill requirements. A number of people worry about job losses stemming from automation and understand the need to upgrade their job skills. Given employee concerns regarding possible job losses and the need for upskilling, it is crucial that agency executives provide options for professional development and gaining the new skills required for emerging technologies. It is vital that employers improve the ways for workers to engage in lifelong learning.

12.7 Conclusion

Advances in process automation and AI are giving government agencies new capabilities to identify system bottlenecks and streamline business and operations processes in ways that can improve business and mission outcomes. Federal legislation has paved the way for municipal governments to affordably go digital. Since digital transformation is inevitable for businesses and local governments around the world, you have the opportunity to reap the benefits of this government modernization. Federal and state government workers are beginning to benefit from a growing army of digital robots designed to streamline agency workloads and quicken the delivery of public services.

Robotic process automation refers to software or processes that enable the automation of routine administrative tasks. RPA technologies emulate human actions and dramatically reduce an organization's low-value workload, freeing up employee time for higher-value work. With RPA, your local government can leverage software that automates government functions across your municipality. Robotic process automation (RPA) is the future of local government, with the power to eliminate thousands of man-hours a year of manual data entry and reduce your municipality's expenses drastically. More information about robotic process automation in government can be found in the books [15-17].

References

[1] H. Kelly, "Public sector robotic process automation: How RPA can transform local governments,"

https://www.govpilot.com/blog/robotic-process-automation-for-local-governments/

[2] M. N. O. Sadiku, P. A. Adekunte, and J. O. Sadiku, "Robotic process automation in government," *International Journal of Trend in Scientific Research and Development*, vol. 9, no. 5, September-October 2025, pp. 170-176.

[3] N. Komitsky, "Putting robotic process automation to work in the federal government,"

https://www.managementconcepts.com/resource/putting-robotic-process-automation-to-work-in-the-federal-government/

[4] A. Raval, "Guidelines for implementing robotic process automation (RPA), from Gururaj Rao, Mahindra Finance, January 2020.

https://www.expresscomputer.in/news/guidelines-for-implementing-robotic-process-automation-rpa-from-gururaj-rao-mahindra-finance/45910/

[5] F. Caltin, "RPA in finance," February 2020,

https://www.plutushealthinc.com/post/rpa-in-finance

[6] "Absolutely everything you need to know about robotic process automation,"

https://www.blueprism.com/guides/robotic-process-automation-rpa/

[7] S. Donnelly, "5 Benefits of robotic process automation in finance," September 2022,

https://www.financealliance.io/5-benefits-of-robotic-process-automation-in-finance/

[8] "Robotic process automation in finance," September 2023,

https://kmbs.konicaminolta.us/blog/robotic-process-automation-in-finance/

[9] "Robotic process automation in finance,"

https://planergy.com/blog/robotic-process-automation-finance/

[10] A. Mishra, "How RPA is optimizing public sector and government processes," April 2023,

https://outworkssolutions.com/technology-blogs/featured/how-rpa-is-optimizing-public-sector-and-government-processes/

[11] D. K. Rehr and D. Munteanu, "The promise of robotic process automation for the public sector," June 2021,

https://cbce.gmu.edu/wp-content/uploads/2021/06/The-Promise-of-RPA-For-The-Public-Sector.pdf

[12] "8 Uses of RPA for government to reduce wasted time," January 2025,

https://provenconsult.com/8-uses-of-rpa-for-government-to-reduce-wasted-time/

[13] M. Headd, "The hidden costs of robotic process automation in government," August 2023,

https://www.govtech.com/opinion/the-hidden-costs-of-robotic-process-automation-in-government

[14] D. M. West, "How robotic process and intelligent automation are altering government performance," November 2021,

https://www.brookings.edu/articles/how-robotic-process-and-intelligent-automation-are-altering-government-performance/

[15] A. Naqvi and J. M. Munoz, *Handbook of Artificial Intelligence and Robotic Process Automation: Policy and Government Applications.* Anthem Press, 2020.

[16] R. Spair, *Comprehensive Guide to Robotic Process Automation (RPA): Tips, Recommendations, and Strategies for Success.* Rick Spair, undated.

[17] D. Valle-Cruz, J. L. Gonzalez-Ruiz, and N. Plata-Cesar, *Handbook of Research on Applied Artificial Intelligence and Robotics for Government Processes.* IGI Global, 2022.

INDEX

www.ingramcontent.com/pod-product-compliance
Lightning Source LLC
LaVergne TN
LVHW051918051126
851858LV00008B/130
9798256009663